Outstanding Dissertations in
ECONOMICS

A Continuing Garland Research Series

A Re-examination of the Gibson Paradox

T. Windsor Fields

Garland Publishing, Inc.
New York & London, 1984

T. Windsor Fields © 1984
All rights reserved

Library of Congress Cataloging in Publication Data

Fields, T. Windsor.
   A re-examination of the Gibson paradox.

   (Outstanding dissertations in economics)
   Originally presented as the author's thesis (Ph.D.—
University of Virginia, 1978) under title: Time series analysis, econometric model construction, and a re-examination of the Gibson paradox.
   Bibliography: p.
   1. Gibson paradox.   I. Title.   II. Series.
HB539.F47   1984   338.5'2   79-53207
ISBN 0-8240-4157-7

All volumes in this series are printed on acid-free, 250-year-life paper.

Printed in the United States of America

TIME SERIES ANALYSIS, ECONOMETRIC MODEL CONSTRUCTION,
AND A RE-EXAMINATION OF THE GIBSON PARADOX

Terry Windsor Fields
Richmond, Virginia

A.B., College of William and Mary, 1971
M.A., University of Michigan, 1972

A Dissertation Presented to the Graduate
Faculty of the University of Virginia
in Candidacy for the Degree of
Doctor of Philosophy

James Wilson Department of Economics

University of Virginia

May 1978

. . . the extraordinary thing is that the
"Gibson Paradox"--as we may fairly call it--
is one of the most completely established
empirical facts within the whole field of
quantitative economics, though theoretical
economists have mostly ignored it. It is
very unlikely indeed that it can be fortuitous,
and it ought, therefore, to be susceptible
of some explanation of a general character.

                              J. M. Keynes
                            <u>A Treatise on Money</u>

ACKNOWLEDGEMENTS

First and foremost, I would like to thank my dissertation supervisor, Bennett T. McCallum, for his initial encouragement to pursue research on the Gibson Paradox and for his countless perceptive comments and suggestions as the work progressed. It is literally true that the beneficial effects of his supervision can be seen on every page of this dissertation. I would also like to thank Richard T. Selden and Peter M. Garber, my second and third readers, and Charles I. Plosser for their thoughtful comments on earlier versions of this work. In addition, I have benefited substantially from a presentation of this material to the Econometrics Workshop at the University of Chicago. Finally, I would like to express my deep appreciation to my wife, Kathi, for her emotional and financial support during my years in graduate school and for the excellent job she has done typing this and all previous drafts of my dissertation. After devoting over two years of my life to this research, I am reluctant to admit the possibility of errors. But if any should remain, they can only be my own.

TABLE OF CONTENTS

Chapter

I.	INTRODUCTION	1
II.	SOME DESCRIPTIVE STATISTICS	4
III.	THE FISHER AND KEYNES-WICKSELL EXPLANATIONS OF THE GIBSON PARADOX	17
IV.	TIME SERIES ANALYSIS AND GRANGER CAUSALITY: AN APPLICATION USING INTEREST RATE AND PRICE LEVEL DATA . . .	28
	APPENDIX TO CHAPTER IV	52
V.	A SMALL-SCALE MACROECONOMETRIC MODEL	57
VI.	TIME SERIES ANALYSIS AND ECONOMETRIC MODEL CONSTRUCTION: AN APPLICATION AND AN EXTENSION	69
VII.	THE GIBSON PARADOX RE-EXAMINED	91
VIII.	CONCLUSION	98
APPENDIX A		105
APPENDIX B		140
APPENDIX C		153
DATA APPENDIX		162
REFERENCES		193

LIST OF TABLES

Table

2-1. SIMPLE CORRELATIONS BETWEEN A LONG-TERM INTEREST RATE OR THE CHANGE IN A LONG-TERM INTEREST RATE AND THE VARIABLE INDICATED, NINE COUNTRIES, VARIOUS PERIODS, ANNUAL DATA 5

2-2. SIMPLE CORRELATIONS BETWEEN A LONG-TERM INTEREST RATE AND AN INDEX OF WHOLESALE PRICES, UNITED STATES, SELECTED PERIODS, 1870 TO 1974, ANNUAL DATA 8

2-3. CORRELATIONS BETWEEN A LONG-TERM INTEREST RATE AND THE LOGARITHM OF A WHOLESALE PRICE INDEX, WITH AND WITHOUT LINEAR TRENDS REMOVED, NINE COUNTRIES, VARIOUS PERIODS, ANNUAL DATA 10

2-4. CORRELATIONS BETWEEN A LONG-TERM INTEREST RATE AND THE LOGARITHM OF A WHOLESALE PRICE INDEX, WITH AND WITHOUT LINEAR TRENDS REMOVED, UNITED STATES, SELECTED PERIODS, 1870 TO 1974, ANNUAL DATA. 13

2-5. CORRELATIONS BETWEEN THE CONSOL YIELD AND THE LOGARITHM OF A WHOLESALE PRICE INDEX, WITH AND WITHOUT LINEAR TRENDS REMOVED, GREAT BRITAIN, SELECTED PERIODS, 1737 TO 1974, ANNUAL DATA 15

3-1. LONG-TERM INTEREST RATE REGRESSED ON THE LOGARITHM OF A WHOLESALE PRICE INDEX AND A PROXY FOR PRICE EXPECTATIONS (π^*), WITH AND WITHOUT LINEAR TRENDS REMOVED, NINE COUNTRIES, VARIOUS PERIODS, ANNUAL DATA 24

4-1. LONG-TERM INTEREST RATE REGRESSED ON THE LOGARITHM OF A WHOLESALE PRICE INDEX, ORDINARY LEAST SQUARES AND COCHRANE-ORCUTT ITERATIVE TECHNIQUE, NINE COUNTRIES, VARIOUS PERIODS, ANNUAL DATA 29

4-2. ARIMA MODELS FITTED TO A LONG-TERM INTEREST RATE AND TO THE LOGARITHM OF A WHOLESALE PRICE INDEX, EIGHT COUNTRIES, SELECTED PERIODS, ANNUAL DATA 39

Table

4-3. CORRELATIONS BETWEEN PREWHITENED R_t AND PREWHITENED LOG(WPI_{t+k}), k = -12, . . . , +12, EIGHT COUNTRIES, SELECTED PERIODS, ANNUAL DATA 45

4-4. POSITIVE CAUSAL RELATIONSHIPS BETWEEN THE INTEREST RATE AND THE PRICE LEVEL IMPLIED BY CROSS CORRELATIONS OF PREWHITENED R_t AND PREWHITENED LOG(WPI_{t+k}), EIGHT COUNTRIES, SELECTED PERIODS, ANNUAL DATA 50

4A-1. LONG-TERM INTEREST RATE REGRESSED ON THE LOGARITHM OF A WHOLESALE PRICE INDEX AND A PROXY FOR PRICE EXPECTATIONS (π^{**}), WITH AND WITHOUT LINEAR TRENDS REMOVED, NINE COUNTRIES, VARIOUS PERIODS, ANNUAL DATA . . . 54

5-1. THREE-STAGE LEAST SQUARES ESTIMATES OF THE MODEL EQUATIONS 68

6-1. ARIMA MODELS FITTED TO THE LOGARITHM OF THE NOMINAL MONEY STOCK, THE LOGARITHM OF NOMINAL GOVERNMENT PURCHASES OF GOODS AND SERVICES, AND THE LOGARITHM OF AN INDEX OF FULL-EMPLOYMENT OUTPUT, UNITED STATES, 1890 TO 1969, ANNUAL DATA 77

6-2. ARIMA MODELS FITTED TO THE LOGARITHM OF REAL GROSS NATIONAL PRODUCT, THE LOGARITHM OF THE IMPLICIT GNP DEFLATOR, AND A LONG-TERM INTEREST RATE, UNITED STATES, 1890 TO 1969, ANNUAL DATA 80

6-3. ESTIMATES OF THE COMPLEX VERSIONS OF THE IMPLIED FINAL EQUATIONS, UNITED STATES, 1890 TO 1969, ANNUAL DATA 88

6-4. RESULTS OF LARGE-SAMPLE LIKELIHOOD RATIO TESTS APPLIED TO FINAL EQUATIONS, UNITED STATES, 1890 TO 1969, ANNUAL DATA 89

7-1. CORRELATIONS BETWEEN Δ LOG y_t, Δ LOG P_t, AND ΔR_t, UNITED STATES, 1890 TO 1969, ANNUAL DATA 93

7-2. COVARIANCES BETWEEN Δ LOG y_t, Δ LOG P_t, AND ΔR_t, ACTUAL AND IMPLIED, UNITED STATES, 1890 TO 1969, ANNUAL DATA 96

CHAPTER I

INTRODUCTION

Over long periods of time and in a number of different countries, interest rates and price levels have tended to move in unison, causing the two series to be highly and positively correlated. So striking and pervasive is this correlation in pre-1930 data that Keynes, in his Treatise on Money (1930, p. 198), called it " . . . one of the most completely established empirical facts within the whole field of quantitative economics." Keynes dubbed this association the "Gibson Paradox" after A. H. Gibson, an English businessman who, in the 1920's, had written several articles for Banker's Magazine calling attention to the high correlation between interest rates and prices evident in 19th and early 20th century British data.

This relationship was considered paradoxical because it appeared to contradict one of the central conclusions of classical monetary theory. According to this theory, interest rates are determined by real factors, such as the marginal productivity of capital and attitudes toward thrift, operating through the market for loanable funds. The price level, on the other hand, is a nominal variable, determined by the stock of money and its velocity relative to the level of real output. Although classical theorists recognized that monetary disequilibrium can generate transitory movements in the rate of interest, the equilibrium rate was thought to be independent of the money stock and hence, given the level of real output, independent of the price level as well. The positive correlation between interest rates and prices appeared to deny this conclusion and was, therefore, considered to be paradoxical.

Naturally enough, there have been numerous attempts over the years to reconcile the Gibson Paradox with classical monetary theory, but none of these has gained universal acceptance. Even those economists who, for various reasons, have not considered the phenomenon paradoxical in the sense of contradicting orthodox theory have been unable to explain it. It seems that what is required is a fresh approach to the study of the phenomenon, and the intent of this dissertation is to provide one.

Of course, the correct explanation of the Gibson Paradox must be consistent with the fundamental statistical characteristics of the phenomenon. Therefore, in Chapter 2, interest rate and price level data for nine countries are examined to determine the primary features of the relationship between the two series. Then, in Chapter 3, the two most prominent explanations of the Paradox are analyzed and found wanting. The simplest alternate hypothesis that provides a rational theoretical basis for the phenomenon is that there exists a strictly bivariate relationship between the interest rate and the price level such that high (low) prices directly "cause" high (low) interest rates and/or vice versa. However, in Chapter 4, this hypothesis is found to be inconsistent with autocorrelation-corrected regressions of interest rates on prices and with the pattern of statistical relationships between these two variables which exists across those countries that exhibit the Paradox. In addition, it is demonstrated that the Gibson Paradox is not an example of spurious correlation and that it has not been caused by coincident trends.

The immediate implication of these findings is that the observed correlation between the interest rate and the price level must result from mutual correlation with a third variable, or perhaps a set of variables. In turn, this suggests a macroeconomic model in which the interest rate and the price level are two of the endogenous variables. If this model can be properly specified, then it may be possible to determine the source of the Gibson Paradox. To this end, a small, and quite orthodox, macroeconomic model is constructed in Chapter 5 and is estimated using annual United States data. Then, in Chapter 6, a relatively new and powerful technique combining traditional econometrics with time series analysis is used to demonstrate that this model is consistent with information contained in the data. In Chapter 7, the model is shown to imply a Gibson Paradox-type relationship between the interest rate and the price level. Moreover, the source of this relationship is found to be innovations in government purchases of goods and services--that is, variations in government purchases that cannot be predicted from the history of the same series.

In the context of the familiar IS-LM, aggregate demand-aggregate supply framework, this explanation of the Gibson Paradox has the simple interpretation of a shifting IS curve which, as is well known, will cause the interest rate and the price level to move in the same direction and, therefore, to be positively correlated--so long as neither the LM nor the aggregate supply schedule is perfectly elastic. Furthermore, this analysis reveals the Gibson Paradox to be not an isolated phenomenon, but rather an element of a larger set of economic relationships, extending, at least, to the level of real income. Finally, a summary of the dissertation is contained in Chapter 8.

CHAPTER II

SOME DESCRIPTIVE STATISTICS

Any analysis of an empirical phenomenon such as the Gibson Paradox must begin with a description of the data. To this end, annual statistics on long-term interest rates and wholesale prices covering various periods were collected for Belgium, Canada, France, Germany, Great Britain, Italy, the Netherlands, Switzerland, and the United States.[1] Table 2-1 presents simple correlation coefficients between the levels and between changes in the levels of these series for each country.[2] Since the United States is widely considered to exhibit the Gibson Paradox,[3] one may conclude, with reference to the correlations between levels of interest rates and levels of wholesale prices, that six of the nine countries examined here are characterized by the

---

[1] This examination was confined to countries for which there exists at least fifty years of published data on both a long-term interest rate (preferably a government bond yield) and an index of wholesale prices. A fifty-year minimum was imposed because a realization of at least this length is required to establish, with any measure of confidence, the time-series properties of a stochastic process. [See Box and Jenkins (1970).] While this restriction is not particularly important in the present context, it will prove to be so in Chapter 4 where causality tests based on time-series properties of the data are employed. Detailed descriptions of each of these series, including actual numbers and sources, are contained in the Data Appendix.

[2] Correlations between interest rates and logarithmic transformations of the wholesale price indexes are included because the first difference of a logarithmic series is a percentage change and, therefore, is comparable to the first difference of an interest rate series.

[3] See, for example, Fisher (1930), Meiselman (1963), Cagan (1965), Sargent (1973a), and Friedman and Schwartz (1976a,b).

TABLE 2-1

SIMPLE CORRELATIONS BETWEEN A LONG-TERM INTEREST RATE OR
THE CHANGE IN A LONG-TERM INTEREST RATE AND THE VARIABLE INDICATED,
NINE COUNTRIES, VARIOUS PERIODS, ANNUAL DATA

Country (Period)	Correlation Between Long-Term Interest Rate and Wholesale Price Index	Correlation Between Long-Term Interest Rate and Log of Wholesale Price Index	Correlation Between Change in Long-Term Interest Rate and Change in Wholesale Price Index	Correlation Between Change in Long-Term Interest Rate and Change in Log of Wholesale Price Index
Belgium (1832-1913)	.09	.08	-.13	-.12
Canada (1900-1974)	.65	.57	.42	.30
France (1798-1974)	.02	.00	.15	.10
Germany (1815-1921)	.59	.75	.14	.24
Gr. Britain (1729-1974)	.80	.74	.49	.20
Italy (1924-1974)	.55	.34	.50	.05
Netherlands (1901-1974)	.71	.62	.48	.28
Switzerland (1921-1974)	.12	.03	.46	.28
United States (1870-1974)	.37	.31	.27	.14

Sources: For all countries except the United States and Germany, the interest rate is the yield on long-term government securities. These yields were taken from A History of Interest Rates by Sidney Homer (Rutgers University Press, 1963) and updated using national publications as well as various issues of International Financial Statistics (International Monetary Fund). From 1870 to 1899 the United States interest rate is Macaulay's adjusted index of American railroad bond yields, and from 1900 to 1970 it is Durand's basic yield on 30-year corporate bonds--both series taken from Long-Term Economic Growth, 1870-1970 (United States Department of Commerce). From 1971 to 1974, the U.S. interest rate is the yield on Moody's Aaa domestic, corporate bonds

TABLE 2-1 (continued)

taken from Business Statistics, 1975 ed., (U.S. Department of Commerce). From 1815 to 1859, the German interest rate is the average annual yield on 3-1/2 and 4% Prussian State bonds. From 1860 to 1869 it is the average annual yield on Bavarian 4% bonds. And from 1870 to 1921 it is an average of high-grade bond yields. All of the German interest rates were taken from A History of Interest Rates. Whenever necessary, yields on different securities were spliced together to form a continuous series.

Wholesale price indexes for all countries except Canada, Great Britain, and the United States were taken from European Historical Statistics 1750-1970 by B. R. Mitchell (The Macmillan Press LTD, 1975) and updated using International Financial Statistics and the Monthly Bulletin of Statistics (United Nations). The Canadian WPI was taken from Historical Statistics of Canada, M. C. Urquhart and K. A. H. Buckley (eds.), (Cambridge University Press, 1965) and International Financial Statistics. The WPI for Great Britain was taken from the Abstract of British Historical Statistics by B. R. Mitchell (Cambridge University Press, 1962), the Second Abstract of British Historical Statistics by B. R. Mitchell and H. G. Jones (Cambridge University Press, 1971), the Annual Abstract of Statistics (Great Britain Central Statistical Office), and International Financial Statistics. The United States WPI was taken from Long-Term Economic Growth, 1870-1970 and Business Statistics, 1975 ed.. Whenever necessary, indexes from separate sources were spliced together to form a continuous series.

See the Data Appendix for a more detailed description of each series.

phenomenon. Only in the data for Belgium, France, and Switzerland does the Paradox fail to appear. First differencing reduces these correlations, on average, by 58% when the wholesale price indexes are transformed logarithmically, and by 28% when they are not. But except for the German and Swiss data, first-differencing appears to preserve, at least roughly, the relative sizes of the correlations. Moreover, only in the case of Belgium does first-differencing produce negative correlations. Of course, the corresponding correlations between the undifferenced series for this country are nearly zero to begin with.

The relatively low correlations for the United States have been shown by Meiselman (1963) to be the result of sharply diverging trends in interest rates and prices during the depression and World War II years. The average annual rise in the wholesale price index was 4.5% between 1932 and 1946, while, over the same period, the interest rate fell steadily from 4.70% to 2.43%. The large, negative correlation during this subperiod causes the correlation for the entire 1870 to 1974 period to be low. However, as Table 2-2 illustrates, subperiods not including the years between 1932 and 1946 have generally been characterized by high, positive correlations between the long-term interest rate and wholesale prices.

One aspect of the phenomenon that is of considerable interest and importance is the extent to which the Gibson Paradox results from coincident long-term trends in interest rates and prices. As a first approximation, this determination can be made by regressing both the interest rate and the price level on a linear time trend and correlating the residuals from these regressions. In effect, this correlation measures the strength of the relationship between the two variables after the

TABLE 2-2

SIMPLE CORRELATIONS BETWEEN A LONG-TERM INTEREST RATE
AND AN INDEX OF WHOLESALE PRICES, UNITED STATES
SELECTED PERIODS, 1870-1974, ANNUAL DATA

Period	Correlation Between R and WPI	Correlation Between R and Log(WPI)
1870-1899	.95	.94
1899-1921	.84	.87
1921-1932	.14	.12
1870-1932	.53	.59
1932-1946	-.77	-.81
1946-1974	.89	.89
1870-1974	.37	.31

Sources: See Data Appendix.

long-run (linear) trend has been removed from each series. However, an implication of an important result[4] proved originally by Frisch and Waugh (1933) is that the correlation between two detrended time series can be obtained simply by regressing either of the raw series on the other and a time trend and then converting the t-statistic associated with the variable of interest into a partial correlation coefficient using the following formula:

$$(\text{Partial correlation coefficient})^2 = \frac{(\text{t-statistic})^2}{(\text{t-statistic})^2 + \text{D.F.}}$$

where D.F. represents the number of degrees of freedom in the regression.

Regressions of this type, employing a linear time trend, were carried out for each of the nine countries mentioned above, and the estimated equations are presented in Table 2-3.[5] Simple and partial correlation coefficients derived from t-statistics associated with the price level variable appear in the last column of the same table. Of the six countries for which the raw data exhibit the Gibson Paradox, detrending eliminates the correlation between the interest rate and the price level only in the case of Italy. Moreover, detrending increases the correlation in the cases of Belgium, France, Germany, Great Britain, Switzerland, and the United States. These results suggest that the high correlations evident in the raw data have not been caused by a persistent

---

[4] This result, proved by Frisch and Waugh (1933), is that a regression of detrended y on detrended x yields precisely the same estimated coefficient and associated t-statistic for the variable x as does a regression of y on x and a time trend.

[5] These estimates are wholly descriptive in nature and, therefore, are not intended to represent behavioral relationships. Consequently, the uniformly low Durbin-Watson statistics associated with these regressions are not indicative of any deficiency. They are simply reflective of the high degree of autocorrelation present in the data. This comment applies as well to the estimates presented in Tables 2-4 and 2-5 below.

TABLE 2-3

CORRELATIONS BETWEEN A LONG-TERM INTEREST RATE AND THE LOGARITHM
OF A WHOLESALE PRICE INDEX, WITH AND WITHOUT LINEAR TRENDS REMOVED,
NINE COUNTRIES, VARIOUS PERIODS, ANNUAL DATA

Country (Period)	Constant	Log of Wholesale Price Index	Time Trend	R^2	D.W.	(Partial) Correlation Between R and Log(WPI)
Belgium (1832-1913)	.31 (.07)	.81 (.76)		.01	.18	.08
	-2.31 (.98)	1.69 (3.20)	-.032 (15.76)	.76	.81	.34
Canada (1900-1974)	-3.33 (2.57)	1.56 (6.00)		.33	.10	.57
	-8.33 (3.54)	2.82 (5.01)	-.033 (2.51)	.38	.12	.51
France (1798-1974)	4.82 (5.98)	.0058 (.04)		.00	.22	.00
	3.61 (4.90)	.84 (5.06)	-.042 (6.91)	.22	.28	.36
Germany (1815-1921)	-.70 (1.70)	1.04 (11.61)		.56	.35	.75
	-.89 (2.21)	1.13 (12.28)	-.004 (2.89)	.59	.40	.77
Great Britain (1729-1974)	-5.43 (10.04)	1.97 (17.29)		.55	.19	.74
	-6.63 (11.53)	2.35 (17.46)	-.005 (4.82)	.59	.21	.75
Italy (1924-1974)	4.62 (9.10)	.17 (2.49)		.11	.44	.34
	5.73 (9.11)	-.18 (1.21)	.052 (2.70)	.23	.51	-.17
Netherlands (1901-1974)	-2.27 (2.34)	1.29 (6.67)		.38	.14	.62
	-1.90 (1.36)	1.19 (3.52)	.004 (.37)	.38	.14	.39

TABLE 2-3 (continued)

Country (Period)	Constant	Wholesale Price Index	Time Trend	R^2	D.W.	(Partial) Correlation Between R and Log(WPI)
Switzerland (1921-1974)	3.57 (1.92)	.081 (.22)		.00	.21	.03
	1.75 (.66)	.53 (.88)	-.013 (.96)	.02	.21	.12
United States (1870-1974)	1.28 (1.42)	.74 (3.26)		.09	.07	.31
	-4.04 (3.67)	2.60 (7.66)	-.036 (6.63)	.37	.14	.60

Note: t-statistics are in parentheses.

Sources: See Data Appendix.

tendency for interest rates and prices to drift in a single direction since, if this were the cause, detrending would eliminate the correlation. In addition, the fact that detrending increases the correlation with some regularity indicates that divergent long-run trends in interest rates and prices often cause the Gibson Paradox to be less pronounced than it would otherwise be. Of course, linear detrending may not be precisely appropriate, but it is a sufficiently close approximation in the present context. Furthermore, it is demonstrated in Chapter 4 that the Gibson Paradox cannot have been caused by coincident trends of any sort. Therefore, the relevant correlations are those between detrended interest rate and price level series. By this criterion, the estimates presented in Table 2-3 indicate that only the data for Italy and Switzerland fail to exhibit the Gibson Paradox.

Following Meiselman (1963), a more detailed examination of the United States data was conducted by dividing the 1870 to 1974 period into four subperiods, each corresponding to an identifiable swing in long-term bond yields. Between 1870 and 1899, yields fell almost steadily, then followed a rising trend up to 1921. The same pattern was repeated in the 1921 to 1946 and 1946 to 1974 subperiods. With one exception, these long swings in bond yields correspond rather closely to long swings in prices in the same direction. The exception is the 1921 to 1946 subperiod that includes those years in which the relationship between interest rates and prices appears to have been atypical, at least in the United States. For each of these subperiods, the interest rate was regressed on the logarithm of the wholesale price index by itself and with a time trend. Estimated equations and correlation coefficients derived from the t-statistics are presented in Table 2-4.

TABLE 2-4

CORRELATIONS BETWEEN A LONG-TERM INTEREST RATE AND THE LOGARITHM
OF A WHOLESALE PRICE INDEX, WITH AND WITHOUT LINEAR TRENDS REMOVED,
UNITED STATES, SELECTED PERIODS, 1870-1974, ANNUAL DATA

Period (Upswing or Downswing in R)	Constant	Log of Wholesale Price Index	Time Trend	R^2	D.W	(Partial) Correlation Between R and Log(WPI)
1870-1899 (Downswing)	-10.78 (9.99)	4.40 (14.21)		.88	.65	.94
	9.37 (1.22)	2.24 (2.59)	-.06 (2.64)	.90	.37	.45
1899-1921 (Upswing)	-1.71 (2.48)	1.55 (8.21)		.76	1.03	.87
	-11.93 (5.35)	.51 (1.99)	.06 (4.70)	.89	1.02	.40
1921-1946 (Downswing)	6.35 (1.44)	-.69 (.60)		.01	.08	-.14
	36.11 (15.89)	-.62 (1.84)	-.11 (15.95)	.92	.84	-.36
1946-1974 (Upswing)	-34.92 (9.08)	8.62 (10.22)		.79	.53	.89
	-49.21 (12.62)	2.60 (1.98)	.14 (5.17)	.90	.54	.36

Note: t-statistics are in parentheses.

Sources: See Data Appendix.

It is immediately apparent that detrending over intervals in which interest rates and prices moved almost exclusively in a single direction eliminates a substantial portion of the correlation between the two series. This result suggests that the Gibson Paradox is, in large part, a consequence of coincident long-period swings in interest rates and prices, with individual swings lasting for decades. It is important to note, however, that the correlation remaining after detrending is not insubstantial, indicating that a short-term correspondence between interest rates and prices is also a significant feature of the Gibson Paradox.[6] The results of this procedure applied to British data are presented in Table 2-5. While these estimates are quite similar to those of Table 2-4, they suggest even more strongly that short-term variations in interest rates and prices are an important aspect of the correlation between the two series.[7]

There are three main conclusions to be drawn from the evidence presented here. The first is that the Gibson Paradox does indeed exist and, furthermore, that it is a fairly widespread phenomenon. Second, long-run trends appear to have little or nothing to do with the Gibson Paradox. In fact, these trends are often in opposite directions, causing the observed correlation to be weaker instead of stronger. And, finally, the Paradox appears to be a composite of short-term and

---

[6]The average of the squared correlation coefficients for the 1870-1899, 1899-1921, and 1946-74 subperiods is .81, indicating that, over these periods, variations in the logarithm of wholesale prices account for 81% of the variation in the interest rate. After detrending within subperiods, variations in prices account, on average, for 16% of the variation in the interest rate.

[7]The average of the squared correlation coefficients is .64, indicating that, between 1737 and 1974, variations in the logarithm of wholesale prices account for 64% of the variation in the interest rate. After detrending within subperiods, variations in prices account, on average, for 26% of the variation in the interest rate.

TABLE 2-5

CORRELATIONS BETWEEN THE CONSOL YIELD AND THE LOGARITHM OF A
WHOLESALE PRICE INDEX, WITH AND WITHOUT LINEAR TRENDS REMOVED,
GREAT BRITAIN, SELECTED PERIODS, 1737 TO 1974, ANNUAL DATA

Period (Upswing or Downswing in R)	Constant	Log of Wholesale Price Index	Time Trend	R^2	D.W	(Partial) Correlation Between R and Log(WPI)
1737-1798 (Upswing)	-15.44 (7.38)	4.34 (9.18)		.58	.69	.76
	-9.78 (2.21)	2.96 (2.77)	.012 (1.45)	.60	.59	.34
1798-1897 (Downswing)	-8.37 (11.22)	2.59 (15.99)		.72	.58	.85
	-.76 (.61)	1.29 (5.70)	-.014 (7.10)	.82	.61	.50
1897-1920 (Upswing)	-5.63 (11.71)	1.97 (18.55)		.94	.45	.97
	-10.87 (14.35)	1.30 (12.05)	.046 (7.36)	.98	1.41	.93
1920-1946 (Downswing)	1.39 (.55)	.51 (.96)		.04	.14	.19
	19.65 (9.41)	.44 (1.91)	-.088 (10.30)	.82	.68	.36
1946-1974 (Upswing)	-46.10 (8.85)	8.75 (10.01)		.79	.44	.89
	-59.55 (10.72)	3.90 (2.66)	.18 (3.78)	.86	.59	.46

Note: t-statistics are in parentheses.

Sources: See Data Appendix.

intermediate-term correlations between interest rates and prices, with the latter accounting for the major share of the overall correlation.

It follows that the correct explanation of the Gibson Paradox ought not to cite coincident trends in interest rates and prices. However, it should be consistent with both short-term and intermediate-term covariations in these two series. And, in the absence of evidence to the contrary, it seems reasonable to assume that these apparently distinct sources of correlation do not require separate explanations. In short, whatever the cause of the Gibson Paradox, any explanation that ignores these characteristics of the phenomenon is likely to be incomplete, if not incorrect.

CHAPTER III

THE FISHER AND KEYNES-WICKSELL EXPLANATIONS
OF THE GIBSON PARADOX

Over the years, there have been numerous attempts to provide a theoretical foundation for the empirical phenomenon known as the Gibson Paradox. Although none of these attempts has gained universal acceptance, two explanations in particular stand out. The more widely accepted of these was originally advanced by Irving Fisher in *The Theory of Interest* (1930), and is intimately related to Fisher's theory of nominal interest rates developed in *Appreciation and Interest* (1896). The second, though decidedly less prominent, explanation is attributed jointly to Keynes (1930) and Wicksell (1935). In what follows, each of these explanations is summarized, and relevant empirical evidence is cited. As it turns out, neither explanation is supported by the data.

The Keynes-Wicksell explanation of the Gibson Paradox centers on the distinction between the natural and the market rate of interest. The natural rate, which is unobservable, is the rate that equates the demand for investment capital and the supply of savings. The market rate, on the other hand, is the rate charged by banks on currently issued loans. If, for some reason, the natural rate should exceed the market rate, then savings would be insufficient to supply all of the loanable funds desired by investors. For a time, banks accommodate this excess demand for loans by allowing their reserve ratios to fall. The direct, though incidental, consequence of this accommodation is an increase in the money stock which stimulates aggregate demand and gives rise to an inflation of indefinite duration. This, of course, is Wicksell's famous "cumulative process." Eventually, however, banks are forced by the pressure of diminishing reserves and dangerously low reserve ratios to increase their rate on loans to the natural rate. At this point, the cumulative process comes to an end. And, in the event that the market rate exceeds the natural rate, bank loans, and hence the money stock and the price level, will fall until accumulating reserves and rising reserve ratios induce banks to lower the loan rate to the natural rate.

According to the traditional view of the Quantity Theory, an increase in the stock of money deriving from, say, an increase in gold production causes bank reserves to rise. Banks respond to this inflow of gold by lowering the market rate of interest and expanding their loans. The consequent rise in prices should produce a negative correlation between the interest rate and the price level--the opposite of the observed relationship. Opponents of the Quantity Theory were quick to point out, however, that the interest rate and the price level are, in fact, positively correlated. Wicksell's distinctive insight, which was reiterated by Keynes and which appeared to reconcile the Gibson Paradox with the Quantity Theory, was to recognize that the natural rate of interest may be subject to autonomous fluctuations. If so, and if banks are slow to adjust the market rate in response, then an imbalance in the market for loanable funds will be created whenever the natural rate changes. This imbalance was thought to be absorbed by the banking system in the form of a steadily increasing or decreasing reserve ratio, thereby producing movements in the money stock and the price level that conform with the eventual change in the market rate of interest.

For example, an autonomous increase in the natural rate of interest gives rise to an excess demand for loans which banks accomodate by allowing their reserve ratios to fall. Eventually, however, banks are forced by the pressure of dwindling reserves to raise the market rate of interst, causing it to move in the same direction as the money stock and the price level. It is in this manner that, in the Keynes-Wicksell explanation, the positive correlation between the interest rate and the price level is alleged to have been produced.

From a theoretical standpoint, there are no flaws in the Keynes-Wicksell explanation of the Gibson Paradox. The major implication of the explanation, however, is at variance with the facts. If Keynes and Wicksell are correct, then changes in the money stock derive primarily from changes in the reserve ratio and not from changes in either the currency-deposit ratio or high-powered money.[1] Cagan (1965), however, has shown that in the pre-1914 period in the United States, variations

---

[1] The reserve ratio test cannot be regarded as definitive, however, since under an international gold standard an increase in the natural rate of interest would give rise to an inflow of gold, which would cause the money stock and the price level to rise along with the market rate of interest. The Gibson Paradox would hold, as would the Keynes-Wicksell explanation of it, even though the rise in the stock of money would have been produced by an increase in high-powered money and not by a decline in the reserve ratio. On the other hand, the Paradox appears to be equally strong in periods in which a gold standard was not in operation, so the Paradox cannot be explained in full by this particular sequence of events. Therefore, to accept the hypothesis that the Gibson Paradox was, under an international gold standard, produced by variations in the natural rate of interest coupled with international gold flows, one would also have to accept the hypothesis that the Paradox has been caused by different sequences of events at different times. But, in the absence of evidence to the contrary, it seems more reasonable to assume that the Paradox has, throughout its history, consistently been produced by only one sequence of events.

in bank reserve ratios did not account for any sizable portion of variations in the money stock. Moreover, Cagan argues, changes in reserve ratios that did occur in this period are better explained by changes in legal requirements and banking practices than by factors related to the demand for and supply of loanable funds. In addition, Jonung (1975) has examined Swedish data for the 1732-1972 period, and his findings are substantially the same as those of Cagan. Furthermore, Schiller and Siegel (1977) have demonstrated, using spectral techniques, that, between 1880 and 1970, the price level in Great Britain was much more closely related to the level of high-powered money than it was to the money multiplier, which is a function of the reserve ratio. In short, the available empirical evidence does not support the Keynes-Wicksell explanation of the Gibson Paradox.

The Fisher explanation of the Gibson Paradox is radically different from the explanation of Keynes and Wicksell. As is well known, Fisher showed that the nominal rate of interest will equal the real rate of interest plus the rate of change in the price level expected over the relevant horizon plus the product of the two. If expectations are formed according to an "adaptive" mechanism and, furthermore, if the mean adjustment lag is very long, then the interest rate will rise slowly throughout upswings in the price level and fall slowly throughout downswings. Therefore, Fisher (1930, p. 441) argued, ". . . at the peak of prices, interest is high, not because the price level is high, but because it has been rising and, at the valley of prices, interest is low, not because the price level is low, but because it has been falling." Nonetheless, high prices tend to be associated with high interest rates and low prices with low interest rates. The Gibson

Paradox appears to be explained.

Fisher's explanation, however, is open to serious criticism on several grounds. First, if his explanation were correct, the Gibson Paradox would have to be considered an "accident of history," for if the time path of the price level had been different, a high positive correlation between the interest rate and the price level might never have occurred. Consider, for example, an economy in which the price level rises continuously but at varying speeds. The interest rate rises when the price level accelerates because inflationary expectations are adjusted upward. By similar reasoning, the interest rate falls when the price level decelerates. In short, the interest rate continuously rises and falls as prices increase monotonically over time. High price levels are not necessarily associated with high interest rates nor are low price levels necessarily associated with low interest rates. It is not at all clear that the Gibson Paradox would characterize such an economy if the Fisher explanation of the phenomenon were, in fact, correct. Fisher, of course, was well aware of this aspect of his explanation, for in The Theory of Interest (pp. 440-1) he wrote:

> The fourth relationship [i.e., the Gibson Paradox] stated above must be, I think, regarded as an accidental consequence . . . . At any rate, it seems impossible to interpret it as representing an independent relationship with any rational theoretical basis. It certainly stands to reason that in the long run a high level of prices due to previous monetary and credit inflation ought not to be associated with any higher rate of interest than the low level before the inflation took place . . . . The price level as such can evidently have no permanent influence on the rate of interest except as a matter of transition from one level or plateau to another. [emphasis in the original]

Nonetheless, Fisher's conclusion that the Gibson Paradox is an "accidental consequence" is difficult to accept. It is hard to believe that any phenomenon persisting over such long periods and in so many different countries could be an accidental consequence of a particular time path of prices.[2]

A second criticism of the Fisher explanation is Cagan's (1965) contention that it requires "implausibly long" lags in the formation of expectations. Sargent (1973a) has provided powerful empirical support for Cagan's criticism by demonstrating that, within the class of autoregressive models, optimal forecasts of changes in the price level require only short distributed lags of past changes. Therefore, long lags in the formation of expectations normally associated with the Fisher explanation are "implausible" because the implied expectational weights associated with past price changes differ significantly from the weights that actually characterize the process by which price changes have been generated. Finally, the evidence most often cited as proof of Fisher's explanation is the high positive correlation typically found between the interest rate and long distributed lags of past price changes, the latter assumed to represent the expected change in prices. However, Macaulay (1938) and Sargent (1973a) have shown that these long distributed lags closely resemble the price level itself, so this correlation is simply the Gibson Paradox in a different guise. It cannot be considered evidence supportive of Fisher's explanation of the same phenomenon.

Using data for each of the nine countries noted in Chapter 2, a somewhat different test of the Fisher explanation was conducted by regressing the rate of interest on the logarithm of wholesale prices

---

[2]To the extent that price levels in different countries move together, the Gibson Paradox would have to be considered one big historical accident rather than many small ones, if the Fisher explanation were correct.

and a Fisherian proxy for the expected rate of change in prices. This proxy, denoted π^*, is a weighted average of the current and the four immediately preceding changes in the logarithm of wholesale prices, the weights being .25, .40, .20, .10, and .05.[3] No lagged price changes earlier than four periods previous were included because it seems reasonable to expect inflationary or deflationary expectations to form within a five-year span. If the Fisher explanation is correct, then π^* should be positively related to the rate of interest. Furthermore, the association between π^* and the interest rate should be stronger than the association between the price level and the interest rate, since only the former are presumed to be linked by any behavioral relationship. Estimated equations[4] and partial correlation coefficients derived from the t-statistics are reported in Table 3-1. The results of these regressions are clearly inconsistent with Fisher's explanation of the Gibson Paradox. The correlation between π^* and the interest rate is zero or negative for each of the nine countries. Detrending causes two of these correlations to become positive, but, in each case, it still is less than the correlation between the interest rate and the price level. These regressions offer further confirmation of the view that a high, positive correlation between the interest rate and a distributed lag of past price changes is not evidence that supports Fisher's explanation of the Gibson Paradox. When account is taken of the positive association between the interest rate and the price level, changes in that level appear entirely unrelated to interest rates, or, at least, unrelated

---

[3] Other weighting schemes were tried, with the same results.

[4] Once again, the low Durbin-Watson statistics are not indicative of any deficiency in the estimated equations, as these equations are descriptive in nature and are not intended to represent behavioral relationships.

TABLE 3-1

LONG-TERM INTEREST RATE REGRESSED ON THE LOGARITHM OF A WHOLESALE PRICE INDEX AND A PROXY FOR PRICE EXPECTATIONS (π^*), WITH AND WITHOUT LINEAR TRENDS REMOVED, NINE COUNTRIES, VARIOUS PERIODS, ANNUAL DATA

Country (Period)	Constant	Log of Wholesale Price Index	π^*	Time Trend	R^2	D.W.	Partial Correlation Between R and Log(WPI)	Partial Correlation Between R and π^*
Belgium (1837-1913)	-5.46 (.97)	2.07 (1.65)	-.17 (.04)		.05	.23	.19	.00
	-3.00 (1.02)	1.83 (2.80)	.17 (.07)	-.032 (14.14)	.75	.85	.31	.01
Canada (1900-1974)	-3.72 (2.80)	1.65 (6.15)	-3.18 (1.29)		.35	.11	.59	-.15
	-11.55 (4.54)	3.63 (5.90)	-6.85 (2.73)	-.049 (3.51)	.44	.14	.57	-.31
France (1803-1974)	3.76 (12.19)	.12 (2.33)	-1.03 (.97)		.03	.16	.18	-.07
	3.39 (13.49)	.49 (8.71)	.32 (.37)	-.021 (9.67)	.38	.24	.56	.03
Germany (1815-1921)	-8.20 (10.18)	2.72 (15.14)	-7.77 (10.01)		.78	.75	.83	-.70
	-8.00 (9.90)	2.70 (15.08)	-7.46 (9.46)	-.0018 (1.71)	.78	.77	.83	-.68

TABLE 3-1 (continued)

Country (Period)	Constant	Log of Wholesale Price Index	π^*	Time Trend	R^2	D.W.	Partial Correlation Between R and Log(WPI)	Partial Correlation Between R and π^*
Great Britain (1729-1974)	-6.10 (10.61)	2.12 (17.35)	-3.87 (3.06)		.57	.19	.74	-.19
	-7.40 (12.26)	2.53 (17.92)	-4.21 (3.49)	-.0050 (5.11)	.61	.21	.76	-.22
Italy (1924-1974)	4.50 (10.17)	.22 (3.61)	-2.51 (4.13)		.35	.62	.46	-.51
	5.14 (8.60)	.017 (.12)	-2.15 (3.35)	.030 (1.57)	.38	.65	.02	-.44
Netherlands (1906-1974)	-2.98 (2.76)	1.45 (6.73)	-4.07 (2.46)		.41	.16	.64	-.29
	-3.30 (2.18)	1.55 (4.19)	-4.21 (2.43)	-.0033 (.31)	.41	.16	.46	-.29
Switzerland (1926-1974)	2.63 (1.35)	.25 (.63)	-1.58 (.61)		.01	.22	.09	-.09
	6.96 (2.20)	-.83 (1.12)	-.87 (.34)	.032 (1.72)	.07	.25	-.16	-.05

TABLE 3-1 (continued)

Country (Period)	Constant	Log of Wholesale Price Index	π*	Time Trend	R^2	D.W.	Partial Correlation Between R and Log(WPI)	Partial Correlation Between R and π*
United States (1870-1974)	.05 (.05)	1.08 (4.58)	-7.51 (3.61)		.20	.12	.41	-.34
	-4.90 (4.63)	2.81 (8.68)	-6.61 (3.79)	-.034 (6.74)	.45	.14	.65	-.35

Note: 1. t-statistics are in parentheses.

2. π* is a weighted average of the current and the four preceding changes in the logarithm of wholesale prices, the weights being .25, .40, .20, .10, and .05.

Sources: See Data Appendix.

in the usual Fisherian sense.

The conclusion to be drawn from all of this is that the two most widely accepted explanations of the Gibson Paradox are unsatisfactory. Moreover, since the "Fisher effect" does not appear to be an important aspect of the correct explanation, then real rates of interest as well as nominal rates should exhibit the Paradox.[5] In the following chapters, an alternate explanation of the Gibson Paradox is developed. This explanation is consistent not only with the empirical regularities described in Chapter 2, but also with the view that the observed correlation between the nominal interest rate and the price level derives from coincident movements in the latter and the real rate of interest.

---

[5] Sargent (1973a) also reaches this conclusion.

CHAPTER IV

TIME SERIES ANALYSIS AND GRANGER CAUSALITY:

AN APPLICATION USING INTEREST RATE AND PRICE LEVEL DATA

The simplest explanation of the Gibson Paradox that attributes the phenomenon to a behavioral relation of some sort is that there exists a strictly bivariate relationship between the interest rate and the price level such that high (low) prices directly "cause" high (low) interest rates and/or vice versa. If this were the correct explanation, then it would be appropriate to estimate the relationship between these two variables simply by regressing one on the other. It will be recalled that regressions of this type, with the interest rate as the left-hand variable, were carried out in Chapter 2 and reported in Table 2-3. For convenience, these have been reproduced in Table 4-1 as the first equation for each country. If these equations are to be given behavioral content, however, then the extremely low Durbin-Watson statistics become a matter of some concern since, as is well known, the usual significance tests on the estimated coefficients are invalid in the presence of autocorrelation. Therefore, each of these equations was re-estimated using the Cochrane-Orcutt iterative technique, the resulting estimates appearing as the second equation for each country in Table 4-1.

It is immediately apparent that the re-estimated equations generally exhibit a much weaker relationship between the interest rate and the price level than do the equations that have not been corrected for autocorrelation. Specifically, t-statistics associated with seven

TABLE 4-1

LONG-TERM INTEREST RATE REGRESSED ON
THE LOGARITHM OF A WHOLESALE PRICE INDEX,
ORDINARY LEAST SQUARES AND COCHRANE-ORCUTT ITERATIVE TECHNIQUE,
NINE COUNTRIES, VARIOUS PERIODS, ANNUAL DATA

Country (Period)	Constant	Log(WPI)	R^2	D.W.	Rho	Correlation Between R and Log(WPI)
Belgium (1832-1913)	.31 (.07)	.81 (.76)	.01	.18		.08
	6.88 (1.81)	-.70 (.84)	.83	2.17	.89	-.09
Canada (1900-1974)	-3.33 (2.57)	1.56 (6.00)	.33	.10		.57
	-.23 (.05)	1.41** (2.87)	.93	1.49	.99	.32
France (1798-1974)	4.82 (5.98)	.0058 (.04)	.00	.22		.00
	3.10 (2.89)	.22 (1.28)	.78	1.90	.73	.10
Germany (1815-1921)	-.70 (1.70)	1.04 (11.61)	.56	.35		.75
	1.73 (2.77)	.52** (4.24)	.88	2.10	.90	.39
Great Britain (1729-1974)	-5.43 (10.04)	1.97 (17.29)	.55	.19		.74
	1.61 (1.38)	.39 (1.57)	.93	1.37	1.12	.10
Italy (1924-1974)	4.62 (9.10)	.17 (2.49)	.11	.44		.34
	3.96 (2.00)	.31 (1.24)	.63	1.56	.85	.18
Netherlands (1901-1974)	-2.27 (2.34)	1.29 (6.67)	.38	.14		.62
	-3.47 (1.30)	.97* (2.26)	.91	1.38	1.02	.26

TABLE 4-1 (continued)

Country (Period)	Constant	Log(WPI)	R^2	D.W.	Rho	Correlation Between R and Log(WPI)
Switzerland (1921-1974)	3.57 (1.92)	.081 (.22)	.00	.21		.03
	-4.46 (1.22)	1.70** (2.43)	.79	1.42	.92	.32
United States (1870-1974)	1.28 (1.42)	.74 (3.26)	.09	.07		.31
	2.17 (1.10)	.60* (1.80)	.94	1.61	.98	.18

Note: 1. t-statistics are in parentheses.

2. * indicates significance at the 5% level (one-tail test).
   ** indicates significance at the 1% level (one-tail test).

3. The second equation for each country was estimated using the Cochrane-Orcutt iterative technique.

Sources: See Data Appendix.

of the nine price level variables decline substantially when the Cochrane-Orcutt procedure is implemented. Moreover, the re-estimated equation for Great Britain exhibits no significant relationship at all. By any measure, this is a striking finding in view of the fact that the correlation between the British interest rate and price level has been the most widely cited example of the Gibson Paradox.

It is extremely difficult to reconcile these results with the hypothesis that the Gibson Paradox is the product of a strictly bivariate relationship. To begin with, this hypothesis cannot explain the existence of the Paradox in British data over the past 250 years. And, furthermore, for six of the nine countries examined, the correlation implied by the Cochrane-Orcutt estimate of the relationship is inconsistent with the correlation actually observed. For example, a strictly bivariate relationship between the German interest rate and price level would have produced a correlation between these two series of only .39 between 1815 and 1921. In fact, the correlation over this period was .75. The strictly bivariate hypothesis cannot account for this higher correlation. Similar arguments can be made regarding Canada, Great Britain, Italy, the Netherlands, and the United States. Of course, it is possible that the relationship between the interest rate and the price level is, in fact, strictly bivariate but that the functional form of this relationship is not semi-log linear. If this were the case, then the estimated equations in Table 4-1 would be misspecified and, therefore, misleading. Consequently, these estimates do not prove that the Gibson Paradox has not been the product of a strictly bivariate relationship. They are, however, highly suggestive that this has not been the case.

One possible explanation of the Gibson Paradox that is suggested by these results is the "spurious regression" phenomenon of Granger and Newbold (1974). Using Monte Carlo techniques, Granger and Newbold showed that it is often possible to find high correlations between time series variables that are independent but highly autocorrelated. Since both the interest rate and the price level have the latter characteristic, it is conceivable that the Gibson Paradox is nothing more than a spurious correlation between these two variables. However, this does not explain the preponderance of positive (as opposed to nonzero) correlations observed across countries unless the two series tend to drift upward or downward together over time. And that the latter has not been the case was suggested by the descriptive statistics of Chapter 2. Nonetheless, this hypothesis merits a more detailed examination, and there exists a type of "causality test" stemming from the work of Granger (1969), Sims (1972), and Haugh (1972), and most recently employed by Feige and Pearce (1976), Frenkel (1976), and Pierce (1977), that is ideally suited for such an examination since it measures the strength of a relationship between two variables after each has been transformed to eliminate all serial correlation and all trend. If a significant relationship between the interest rate and the price level can still be detected after such a transformation has been applied to each series, then the spurious regression and coincident trend hypotheses (separately or in conjunction with one another) will have been discredited.

The test to be employed here is based on Granger's (1969) definition of causality, which can be expressed as follows: Let A be an information set which consists of $(P_t, R_t;\ t = 0, \pm 1, \pm 2, \ldots)$

where P_t is the current price level and R_t is the current interest rate. Define $\bar{A}_t$ and $\bar{\bar{A}}_t$ as

$$\bar{A}_t = (P_{t-j}, R_{t-j}; j = 1, 2, 3, \ldots)$$
$$\text{and } \bar{\bar{A}}_t = (P_{t-j}, R_{t-j}; j = 0, 1, 2, \ldots).$$

The information sets $\bar{P}_t$, $\bar{\bar{P}}_t$, $\bar{R}_t$, and $\bar{\bar{R}}_t$ are defined similarly.[1] Finally, let $P^*(P_t|B)$ denote the minimum mean square error (MSE) prediction of P_t given the information set B, and let $\sigma^2(P_t|B)$ be the corresponding minimum MSE. R is said to "cause" P relative to the set A if

$$\sigma^2(P_t|\bar{A}_t) < \sigma^2(P_t|\bar{P}_t).$$

And R is said to "cause P instantaneously" relative to the set A if

$$\sigma^2(P_t|\bar{A}_t, \bar{\bar{R}}_t) < \sigma^2(P_t|\bar{A}_t).$$

Causality from P to R is defined in the same manner.

Less formally, R causes P in Granger's sense if, and only if, optimum predictions of P_t conditional on previous values of P and R are significantly better than optimum predictions conditional on previous values of P alone. And, R causes P instantaneously if, and only if, optimum predictions of P_t conditional on contemporaneous R in addition to previous values of R and P are significantly better than optimum predictions conditional on previous values of R and P alone.[2] These statements also hold with R and P reversed.

The Haugh (1972) procedure for detecting bivariate relationships

---

[1] For example, $\bar{P}_t = (P_{t-j}; j = 1, 2, 3, \ldots)$.

[2] Alternate, and perhaps more suggestive, terminology is as follows: If R causes P in Granger's sense, then R is said to be a "leading indicator of P," and P is said to be "endogenous" with respect to R. If, in addition, P does not cause R, then causality is said to be "unidirectional" from R to P, and R is said to be "exogenous" with respect to P. See Pierce (1977).

that are causal in Granger's sense builds on the time series methodology developed by Box and Jenkins (1970). In this approach, each observed time series is assumed to be a realization of a specific, but unknown, member of the class of stochastic processes known as autoregressive integrated moving average (ARIMA) processes. These are of the form

$$\phi(L)(1-L)^d x_t = a_o + \theta(L) a_t,$$

where L is a lag operator such that $L^n x_t = x_{t-n}$, ϕ and θ are polynomials in L with roots outside the unit circle, a_o is a constant term, a_t is a white noise process[3], and d is the number of times x_t must be differenced to induce covariance stationarity.[4] If the autoregressive and moving average lag polynomials [$\phi(L)$ and $\theta(L)$, respectively] have degrees p and q, then the stochastic process generating x_t is said to be ARIMA (p,d,q).

As a first step toward determining the stochastic process generating an observed time series, Box and Jenkins show how to identify a subclass of ARIMA processes containing individual members which have theoretical autocorrelation and partial autocorrelation functions that are consistent with those characterizing the observed series. Models representing the processes in this subclass are then estimated and subjected to several tests of model adequacy. The first set of tests arises from the fact that if a model is an adequate representation of the process generating an observed series, then the model residuals will be white noise and, therefore, uncorrelated. Consequently, the presence

---

[3] A "white noise" process is a sequence of uncorrelated random variables with zero mean and constant, finite variance.

[4] A stochastic process is said to be "covariance stationary" if it has a constant, finite mean and an autocorrelation function that is independent of historical time.

of serial correlation in the estimated residuals is indicative of model inadequacy. Box and Jenkins suggest two procedures for detecting whatever serial correlation may exist. First, the residual autocorrelations at various lags can be tested for significance individually. This is done by comparing each autocorrelation with its approximate standard error of $1/\sqrt{n}$, where n is the sample size. Model inadequacy is indicated if more of these autocorrelations exceed twice their standard error than would be expected by chance. Second, the first K autocorrelations can be tested for significance as a group by calculating the Box-Pierce statistic. This statistic, denoted Q, is

$$Q = n \sum_{k=1}^{K} r_k^2(\hat{a}),$$

where $r_k(\hat{a})$ is the autocorrelation of the model residuals at lag k. If the fitted model is an adequate representation of the underlying stochastic process, Q will be approximately distributed $\chi^2(K-p-q)$. Therefore, should the calculated value of Q exceed the appropriate χ^2 value, then model inadequacy is indicated.

The other important diagnostic check, overfitting, involves estimating a model more elaborate than the one believed to be correct. The two models are then compared on the basis of significance of estimated parameters and diagnostic checks applied to model residuals. If the two appear to fit the data equally well, then, by the law of parsimony, the simpler one is chosen. In addition, if the simpler model is "nested" in the more elaborate one, as is usually the case with overfits, a likelihood ratio test[5] can be used to enable one to

---

[5]For a description of this test see Zellner and Palm (1974).

select the more representative model. Normally, these procedures will lead to at least one acceptable model from within the subclass of ARIMA processes identified at the preliminary stage. But, if they do not, then the search must be expanded to include processes outside the original subclass, thereby initiating another cycle of identification, estimation, and verification.

To return to the earlier discussion, it will be recalled that R causes P in Granger's sense if and only if previous values of R (that is, $\bar{R}_t$) can be used to improve predictions of P_t conditional on previous values of P (that is, conditional on $\bar{P}_t$). This suggests that causality from R to P can be assessed by correlating $\bar{R}_t$ with the part of P_t that cannot be explained from its own history. But this part of P_t is precisely equivalent to the contemporaneous residual from the univariate ARIMA model fitted to P. This is so because a properly fitted ARIMA model efficiently utilizes all of the information contained in a sequence of observations on a time series variable. Therefore, to implement this test for Granger causality, one needs to "prewhiten" the P series by obtaining the $\hat{u}_t$'s from the following model:

$$\hat{\phi}_P(L)P_t = \hat{u}_o + \hat{\theta}_P(L)\hat{u}_t.$$

Similarly, to test for causality from P to R, one needs to obtain the $\hat{v}_t$'s from the univariate ARIMA model fitted to R, which is

$$\hat{\phi}_R(L)R_t = \hat{v}_o + \hat{\theta}_R(L)\hat{v}_t.$$

Unfortunately, correlations of $\bar{R}_t$ with $\hat{u}_t$ and $\bar{P}_t$ with $\hat{v}_t$ are misleading due to serial correlation present in the series that is not prewhitened.[6] However, Haugh (1972) has shown how to circumvent this

---

[6] For a discussion of this point, see Bartlett (1935).

problem and, at the same time, test for causality in both directions simultaneously. This is done by prewhitening both R and P using the appropriate univariate ARIMA models and cross-correlating the model residuals, that is, $\hat{u}_t$ and $\hat{v}_t$. Under the null hypothesis that R and P are not causally related, the residual cross correlations are asymptotically distributed as independent normal variates with zero mean and standard deviation $1/\sqrt{n}$. Furthermore, the statistic

$$S = n \sum_{k=1}^{M} \hat{r}_k^2,$$

where $\hat{r}_k$ is the correlation between $\hat{u}_{t+k}$ and $\hat{v}_t$, is distributed χ^2 with M degrees of freedom.

The appearance of cross correlations exceeding twice their standard error is indicative of a causal relationship between R and P, and the location of these nonzero $\hat{r}_k$'s determines the direction of causality. For example, $\hat{r}_k \neq 0$ for some $k > 0$ indicates that R causes P with a lag equal to the value of k. A second, but complementary, test for causality employs the statistic S. The null hypothesis that R does not cause P can be rejected at the α% level of significance if

$$n \sum_{k=1}^{M} \hat{r}_k^2 > \chi_\alpha^2(M),$$

where $\chi_\alpha^2(M)$ is the upper α-percentage point of the χ^2 distribution with M degrees of freedom. Similarly, the null hypothesis that P does not cause R can be rejected at the α% level of significance if

$$n \sum_{k=-1}^{-M} \hat{r}_k^2 > \chi_\alpha^2(M).$$

Finally, instantaneous causality between R and P is indicated if the absolute value of $\hat{r}_o$, the correlation at lag zero, exceeds $2/\sqrt{n}$. However, the direction of causality in the instantaneous case is indeterminate.

Causality tests of this type were conducted using long-term interest rate and wholesale price data for Belgium, Canada, France, Germany, Italy, the Netherlands, Switzerland, and the United States.[7] For each country, univariate ARIMA models were fitted to the interest rate and price level variables using the techniques of Box and Jenkins.[8] These models are shown in Table 4-2, while the estimated autocorrelation and partial autocorrelation functions appear in Appendix A.[9] Residuals from these models were then correlated at lags of from zero to twelve years in each direction. The resulting cross-correlation functions are displayed in Table 4-3 along with approximate standard errors and calculated X^2 statistics. Causal relationships revealed by these functions include a small number implied by significantly negative cross correlations. But since only positive correlations have any relevance for the Gibson Paradox, only these are reported in Table 4-4, which summarizes the results of these tests.

For six of the eight countries examined, the prewhitened interest rate and prewhitened price level series are significantly and positively correlated in spite of the fact that each is non-autocorrelated and

---

[7]Great Britain was excluded because ARIMA models for the British consol yield and an index of wholesale prices that passed the required diagnostic checks could not be found.

[8]The computer program used is *Estimate* (version: 5/1/75), developed by Charles R. Nelson at the Graduate School of Business, University of Chicago.

[9]In the case of France, no model was found which adequately describes movements in wholesale prices over the entire sample period. It was, therefore, necessary to divide the period in two and fit separate models for each subperiod. The year 1914 proved to be a satisfactory breaking point, coinciding as it did with the demise of the international gold standard, the start of World War I, and the transition in France from relatively stable prices to a prolonged period of rapid inflation.

TABLE 4-2

ARIMA MODELS FITTED TO A LONG-TERM INTEREST RATE
AND TO THE LOGARITHM OF A WHOLESALE PRICE INDEX,
EIGHT COUNTRIES, SELECTED PERIODS, ANNUAL DATA

BELGIUM

<u>Variable</u>: Logarithm of a Wholesale Price Index (Log WPI)
<u>Sample Period</u>: 1832 to 1913
<u>Time Series Process</u>: ARIMA (5,1,5) with ϕ_1, ϕ_3, ϕ_4, θ_1, θ_2, θ_3, and and θ_4 suppressed
<u>Fitted Model</u>:

$$(1 + \underset{(3.76)}{.194}L^2 + \underset{(21.41)}{.844}L^5) \, \Delta \log WPI_t = \underset{(.70)}{.00671} + (1 + \underset{(21.26)}{.904}L^5)\hat{a}_t$$

R^2 = .18
D.F. = 77
$\hat{\sigma}^2$ = .00206

Box-Pierce Statistics	Degrees of Freedom	Critical Q Values (10% level of sig.)
Q(12) = 9.9	9	14.7
Q(24) = 19.6	21	29.6

<u>Variable</u>: Yield on Long-Term Government Securities (R)
<u>Sample Period</u>: 1831 to 1913
<u>Time Series Process</u>: ARIMA (0,1,0)
<u>Fitted Model</u>:

$$\Delta R_t = \underset{(.76)}{-.0313} + \hat{a}_t$$

D.F. = 81
$\hat{\sigma}^2$ = .140

Box-Pierce Statistics	Degrees of Freedom	Critical Q Values (10% level of sig.)
Q(12) = 8.0	12	18.5
Q(24) = 12.6	24	33.2

CANADA

<u>Variable</u>: Logarithm of a Wholesale Price Index (Log WPI)
<u>Sample Period</u>: 1867 to 1974
<u>Time Series Process</u>: ARIMA (0,1,1)
<u>Fitted Model</u>:

$$\Delta \log WPI_t = \underset{(1.70)}{.0170} + (1 + \underset{(5.51)}{.473}L)\hat{a}_t$$

R^2 = .18
D.F. = 105
$\hat{\sigma}^2$ = .00492

Box-Pierce Statistics	Degrees of Freedom	Critical Q Values (10% level of sig.)
Q(12) = 8.6	11	17.3
Q(24) = 16.1	23	32.0

TABLE 4-2 (continued)

CANADA

Variable: Yield on Long-Term Government Securities (R)
Sample Period: 1900 to 1974
Time Series Process: ARIMA (0,1,1)
Fitted Model:

$$\Delta R_t = \underset{(1.48)}{.0798} + (1 + \underset{(2.10)}{.260L})\hat{a}_t$$

$R^2 = .06$
D.F. = 72
$\hat{\sigma}^2 = .136$

Box-Pierce Statistics	Degrees of Freedom	Critical Q Values (10% level of sig.)
Q(12) = 8.1	11	17.3
Q(24) = 13.9	23	32.0

FRANCE

Variable: Logarithm of a Wholesale Price Index (Log WPI)
Sample Period: 1798 to 1914
Time Series Process: ARIMA (0,1,0)
Fitted Model:

$$\Delta \log WPI_t = \underset{(.63)}{-.00369} + \hat{a}_t$$

D.F. = 115
$\hat{\sigma}^2 = .00403$

Box-Pierce Statistics	Degrees of Freedom	Critical Q Values (10% level of sig.)
Q(12) = 8.0	12	18.5
Q(24) = 16.3	24	33.2

Variable: Log WPI
Sample Period: 1914 to 1974
Time Series Process: ARIMA (1,1,0)
Fitted Model:

$$(1 - \underset{(4.32)}{.491L}) \Delta \log WPI_t = \underset{(2.44)}{.0541} + \hat{a}_t$$

$R^2 = .23$
D.F. = 58
$\hat{\sigma}^2 = .0223$

Box-Pierce Statistics	Degrees of Freedom	Critical Q Values (10% level of sig.)
Q(12) = 8.5	11	17.3
Q(24) = 21.7	23	32.0

TABLE 4-2 (continued)

FRANCE

Variable: Yield on Long-Term Government Securities (R)
Sample Period: 1798 to 1974
Time Series Process: ARIMA (0,1,1)
Fitted Model:

$$\Delta R_t = -.0994 + (1 + .302L)\hat{a}_t$$
$$(.68) (4.94)$$

$R^2 = .04$
D.F. = 174
$\hat{\sigma}^2 = 2.24$

Box-Pierce Statistics	Degrees of Freedom	Critical Q Values (10% level of sig.)
Q(12) = 2.1	11	17.3
Q(24) = 6.1	23	32.0

GERMANY

Variable: Logarithm of a Wholesale Price Index (Log WPI)
Sample Period: 1792 to 1921
Time Series Process: ARIMA (0,1,1)
Fitted Model:

$$\Delta \log WPI_t = .0217 + (1 + .612L)\hat{a}_t$$
$$(1.20) (8.05)$$

$R^2 = .27$
D.F. = 127
$\hat{\sigma}^2 = .0164$

Box-Pierce Statistics	Degrees of Freedom	Critical Q Values (10% level of sig.)
Q(12) = 5.2	11	17.3
Q(24) = 11.7	23	32.0

Variable: Yield on Long-Term Government Securities and High-Grade Bonds (R)
Sample Period: 1815 to 1921
Time Series Process: ARIMA (0,1,0)
Fitted Model:

$$\Delta R_t = .0191 + \hat{a}_t$$
$$(.82)$$

D.F. = 105
$\hat{\sigma}^2 = .0566$

Box-Pierce Statistics	Degrees of Freedom	Critical Q Values (10% level of sig.)
Q(12) = 7.0	12	18.5
Q(24) = 13.0	24	33.2

TABLE 4-2 (continued)

ITALY

Variable: Logarithm of a Wholesale Price Index (Log WPI)
Sample Period: 1861 to 1974
Time Series Process: ARIMA (1,1,0)
Fitted Model:

$$(1 - .667L) \Delta \log WPI_t = .0197 + \hat{a}_t$$
$$(9.29)(1.45)$$

$R^2 = .43$
D.F. = 111
$\hat{\sigma}^2 = .0200$

Box-Pierce Statistics	Degrees of Freedom	Critical Q Values (10% level of sig.)
Q(12) = 5.5	11	17.3
Q(24) = 11.4	23	32.0

Variable: Yield on Long-Term Government Securities (R)
Sample Period: 1924 to 1974
Time Series Process: ARIMA (0,1,0)
Fitted Model:

$$\Delta R_t = .0742 + \hat{a}_t$$
$$(.82)$$

D.F. = 49
$\hat{\sigma}^2 = .412$

Box-Pierce Statistics	Degrees of Freedom	Critical Q Values (10% level of sig.)
Q(12) = 8.2	12	18.5
Q(24) = 10.1	24	33.2

NETHERLANDS

Variable: Logarithm of a Wholesale Price Index (Log WPI)
Sample Period: 1901 to 1974
Time Series Process: ARIMA (1,1,0)
Fitted Model:

$$(1 - .555L) \Delta \log WPI_t = .0126 + \hat{a}_t$$
$$(5.57)(1.18)$$

$R^2 = .30$
D.F. = 71
$\hat{\sigma}^2 = .00805$

Box-Pierce Statistics	Degrees of Freedom	Critical Q Values (10% level of sig.)
Q(12) = 11.1	11	17.3
Q(24) = 22.0	23	32.0

TABLE 4-2 (continued)

NETHERLANDS

<u>Variable</u>: Yield on Long-Term Government Securities (R)
<u>Sample Period</u>: 1814 to 1974
<u>Time Series Process</u>: ARIMA (2,1,2) with ϕ_1 and θ_1 suppressed
<u>Fitted Model</u>:

$$(1 + .908L^2) \Delta R_t = .0290 + (1 + .722L^2)\hat{a}_t$$
$$\quad (10.54) \qquad\qquad (.57) \quad\; (5.68)$$

$R^2 = .07$
D.F. = 157
$\hat{\sigma}^2 = .143$

Box-Pierce Statistics	Degrees of Freedom	Critical Q Values (10% level of sig.)
Q(12) = 11.7	10	16.0
Q(24) = 20.8	22	30.8

SWITZERLAND

<u>Variable</u>: Logarithm of a Wholesale Price Index (Log WPI)
<u>Sample Period</u>: 1921 to 1974
<u>Time Series Process</u>: ARIMA (1,1,0)
<u>Fitted Model</u>:

$$(1 - .577L) \Delta \log WPI_t = .00494 + \hat{a}_t$$
$$\quad (5.15) \qquad\qquad\quad (.53)$$

$R^2 = .28$
D.F. = 51
$\hat{\sigma}^2 = .00475$

Box-Pierce Statistics	Degrees of Freedom	Critical Q Values (10% level of sig.)
Q(12) = 6.5	11	17.3
Q(24) = 12.4	23	32.0

<u>Variable</u>: Yield on Long-Term Government Securities (R)
<u>Sample Period</u>: 1916 to 1974
<u>Time Series Process</u>: ARIMA (2,1,0) with ϕ_1 suppressed
<u>Fitted Model</u>:

$$(1 + .470L^2) \Delta R_t = .0372 + \hat{a}_t$$
$$\quad (3.51) \qquad\qquad (.61)$$

$R^2 = .18$
D.F. = 56
$\hat{\sigma}^2 = .208$

Box-Pierce Statistics	Degrees of Freedom	Critical Q Values (10% level of sig.)
Q(12) = 6.8	11	17.3
Q(24) = 9.4	23	32.0

TABLE 4-2 (continued)

UNITED STATES

Variable: Logarithm of a Wholesale Price Index (Log WPI)
Sample Period: 1870 to 1974
Time Series Process: ARIMA (1,1,0)
Fitted Model:

$$(1 - .279L) \Delta \log WPI_t = .00870 + \hat{a}_t$$
$$\quad\quad (2.89) \quad\quad\quad\quad\quad\quad (1.06)$$

$R^2 = .08$
D.F. = 102
$\hat{\sigma}^2 = .00700$

Box-Pierce Statistics	Degrees of Freedom	Critical Q Values (10% level of sig.)
Q(12) = 10.2	11	17.3
Q(24) = 19.9	23	32.0

Variable: Yield on Long-Term Corporate Bonds (R)
Sample Period: 1870 to 1974
Time Series Process: ARIMA (1,1,0)
Fitted Model:

$$(1 - .183L) \Delta R_t = .0144 + \hat{a}_t$$
$$\quad\quad (1.75) \quad\quad\quad\quad (.49)$$

$R^2 = .03$
D.F. = 102
$\hat{\sigma}^2 = .0889$

Box-Pierce Statistics	Degrees of Freedom	Critical Q Values (10% level of sig.)
Q(12) = 14.6	11	17.3
Q(24) = 18.6	23	32.0

Note:
1. t-statistics are in parentheses.
2. L is a lag operator such that $L^n x_t = x_{t-n}$.
3. Q(K) is distributed χ^2 with K - p - q degrees of freedom, where p + q equals the number of autoregressive and moving average parameters estimated.

Sources: See Data Appendix.

TABLE 4-3

CORRELATIONS BETWEEN PREWHITENED R_t AND PREWHITENED $\text{LOG}(\text{WPI}_{t+k})$,
$k = -12,\ldots,+12$, EIGHT COUNTRIES, SELECTED PERIODS, ANNUAL DATA

BELGIUM (1832-1913)

Correlation at lag zero: $-.08$
$2(\text{s.e.})$: $.22$

k:	1	2	3	4	5	6	7	8	9	10	11	12	$S = n\Sigma \hat{r}^2(k)$	$\chi^2_{.05}(12)$
$\hat{r}_k$:	-.13	.06	-.09	-.29	.15	.06	.18	.15	.02	.12	-.11	-.10	18.68	21.03

k:	-1	-2	-3	-4	-5	-6	-7	-8	-9	-10	-11	-12		
$\hat{r}_k$:	.53*	-.01	-.13	-.15	-.18	.05	.24*	.02	.10	.07	-.10	.12	36.66	21.03
$2(\text{s.e.})$:	.22	.23	.23	.23	.23	.23	.23	.23	.24	.24	.24	.24		

CANADA (1900-1974)

Correlation at lag zero: $.22$
$2(\text{s.e.})$: $.23$

k:	1	2	3	4	5	6	7	8	9	10	11	12	$S = n\Sigma \hat{r}^2(k)$	$\chi^2_{.05}(12)$
$\hat{r}_k$:	-.18	.10	-.09	.08	.13	-.12	.08	.07	-.03	.06	-.11	-.04	8.71	21.03

k:	-1	-2	-3	-4	-5	-6	-7	-8	-9	-10	-11	-12		
$\hat{r}_k$:	.31*	-.01	.12	.08	-.01	.02	-.09	-.05	.16	-.03	-.03	.21	14.74	21.03
$2(\text{s.e.})$:	.23	.24	.24	.24	.24	.24	.24	.25	.25	.25	.25	.25		

TABLE 4-3 (continued)

FRANCE (1798-1914)

Correlation at lag zero: -.02
2(s.e.): .19

k:	1	2	3	4	5	6	7	8	9	10	11	12	$S = n\Sigma \hat{r}^2(k)$	$\chi^2_{.05}(12)$
$\hat{r}_k$:	.11	-.05	-.13	.13	-.16	-.10	.05	-.40	.08	-.09	-.01	-.06	30.71	21.03

k:	-1	-2	-3	-4	-5	-6	-7	-8	-9	-10	-11	-12		
$\hat{r}_k$:	.03	.03	.08	.09	.15	.02	.06	.25*	-.13	.11	-.01	-.29	25.35	21.03
2(s.e.):	.19	.19	.19	.19	.19	.19	.19	.19	.19	.19	.20	.20		

FRANCE (1914-1974)

Correlation at lag zero: .35*
2(s.e.): .26

k:	1	2	3	4	5	6	7	8	9	10	11	12	$S = n\Sigma \hat{r}^2(k)$	$\chi^2_{.05}(12)$
$\hat{r}_k$:	.10	-.11	.10	.08	-.02	-.12	-.20	.15	.03	-.22	-.06	.15	11.47	21.03

k:	-1	-2	-3	-4	-5	-6	-7	-8	-9	-10	-11	-12		
$\hat{r}_k$:	-.05	.05	.08	-.31	.18	.09	-.18	.09	.05	-.04	-.02	-.26	15.64	21.03
2(s.e.):	.26	.26	.26	.27	.27	.27	.27	.28	.28	.28	.28	.29		

TABLE 4-3 (continued)

GERMANY (1815-1921)

Correlation at lag zero: .18
2(s.e.): .19

k:	1	2	3	4	5	6	7	8	9	10	11	12	$S = n\Sigma\hat{r}^2(k)$	$\chi^2_{.05}(12)$
$\hat{r}_k$:	.34*	-.14	.01	.08	.21*	.38*	.00	.03	.02	-.04	-.04	.06	35.86	21.03

k:	-1	-2	-3	-4	-5	-6	-7	-8	-9	-10	-11	-12		
$\hat{r}_k$:	.20*	.18	.07	.27*	.12	-.02	-.04	-.06	.09	.23*	-.12	.06	26.42	21.03
2(s.e.):	.20	.20	.20	.20	.20	.20	.20	.20	.20	.20	.21	.21		

ITALY (1924-1974)

Correlation at lag zero: .02
2(s.e.): .28

k:	1	2	3	4	5	6	7	8	9	10	11	12	$S = n\Sigma\hat{r}^2(k)$	$\chi^2_{.05}(12)$
$\hat{r}_k$:	-.13	-.18	-.12	.16	.01	.01	-.03	.02	.18	-.01	-.23	.05	8.94	21.03

k:	-1	-2	-3	-4	-5	-6	-7	-8	-9	-10	-11	-12		
$\hat{r}_k$:	-.05	.11	.12	-.01	-.01	.07	.05	-.06	.04	.05	.05	.08	2.66	21.03
2(s.e.):	.28	.29	.29	.29	.30	.30	.31	.31	.31	.32	.32	.32		

TABLE 4-3 (continued)

NETHERLANDS (1901-1974)

Correlation at lag zero: .23*
2(s.e.): .23

k:	1	2	3	4	5	6	7	8	9	10	11	12	$S = n\Sigma\hat{r}^2(k)$	$\chi^2_{.05}(12)$
$\hat{r}_k$:	-.07	-.21	-.16	.14	.08	.03	.04	.05	.00	-.03	-.03	-.27	13.13	21.03
k:	-1	-2	-3	-4	-5	-6	-7	-8	-9	-10	-11	-12		
$\hat{r}_k$:	.08	.07	.11	.18	.08	.07	-.11	-.06	-.08	-.09	.12	.00	8.15	21.03
2(s.e.):	.24	.24	.24	.24	.24	.24	.25	.25	.25	.25	.25	.26		

SWITZERLAND (1921-1974)

Correlation at lag zero: .25
2(s.e.): .27

k:	1	2	3	4	5	6	7	8	9	10	11	12	$S = n\Sigma\hat{r}^2(k)$	$\chi^2_{.05}(12)$
$\hat{r}_k$:	.09	.09	-.04	.05	.18	.24	.20	.21	.03	-.17	.02	.11	12.55	21.03
k:	-1	-2	-3	-4	-5	-6	-7	-8	-9	-10	-11	-12		
$\hat{r}_k$:	.10	-.10	.02	-.03	-.02	.16	.03	.10	-.19	-.05	.07	.08	5.73	21.03
2(s.e.):	.28	.28	.28	.28	.29	.29	.29	.30	.30	.31	.31	.31		

TABLE 4-3 (continued)

UNITED STATES (1870-1974)

Correlation at lag zero: .07
2(s.e.): .20

k:	1	2	3	4	5	6	7	8	9	10	11	12	$S = n\Sigma \hat{r}^2(k)$	$\chi^2_{.05}(12)$
$\hat{r}_k$:	-.15	.12	-.08	.15	.22*	.00	-.01	-.02	.11	.07	-.09	-.05	14.80	21.03
k:	-1	-2	-3	-4	-5	-6	-7	-8	-9	-10	-11	-12		
$\hat{r}_k$:	.30*	.09	.05	.13	.03	.05	.05	-.06	.09	.06	-.08	.21*	19.68	21.03
2(s.e.):	.20	.20	.20	.20	.20	.20	.20	.20	.21	.21	.21	.21		

Note: The prewhitened series are the residuals from the ARIMA models fitted to R and log(WPI) shown in Table 4-1. $\hat{r}_k$ is the correlation between R_t and $\text{Log}(\text{WPI}_{t+k})$. Positive correlations equalling or exceeding twice their standard error (s.e.) of $1/\sqrt{n}$, n being the number of observations, are marked with an asterisk (*). The statistic S is approximately distributed χ^2 with 12 degrees of freedom, and $\chi^2_{.05}(12)$ is its critical value at the 5% level of significance.

TABLE 4-4

POSITIVE CAUSAL RELATIONSHIPS
BETWEEN THE INTEREST RATE AND THE PRICE LEVEL
IMPLIED BY CROSS CORRELATIONS
OF PREWHITENED R_t AND PREWHITENED $LOG(WPI_{t+k})$,
EIGHT COUNTRIES, SELECTED PERIODS, ANNUAL DATA

Country (Periods)	Positive Instantaneous Causality	R "Causes" P Positively	P "Causes" R Positively
Belgium (1832-1913)			X(1,7)
Canada (1900-1974)			X(1)
France (1798-1914)			X(8)
France (1914-1974)	X(0)		
Germany (1815-1921)		X(1,5,6)	X(1,4,10)
Italy (1924-1974)			
Netherlands (1901-1974)	X(0)		
Switzerland (1921-1974)			
United States (1870-1974)		X(5)	X(1,12)

Note: $\hat{r}_k$ is the correlation between prewhitened R_t and prewhitened $Log(WPI_{t+k})$. R was found to cause P positively whenever $\hat{r}_k > 0$ and $\hat{r}_k \geq$ twice its standard error for at least one $k > 0$. P was found to cause R positively whenever $\hat{r}_k > 0$ and $\hat{r}_k \geq$ twice its standard error for at least one $k < 0$. Positive instantaneous causality is indicated by $\hat{r}_0 > 0$ and $\hat{r}_0 \geq$ twice its standard error. The number(s) in parentheses is (are) the absolute value(s) of k for which $\hat{r}_k$ is significantly positive--that is, the length of the lag, in years, in the indicated causal relationship.

trend-free by construction. Moreover, the absence of any relationship in the Swiss data is not particularly surprising since Switzerland does not unambiguously exhibit the Paradox to begin with. (See Tables 2-1 and 4-1.) These results demonstrate conclusively that the Gibson Paradox is not an example of spurious correlation since, if it were, the causality tests employed here would not have detected any significant relationships. By the same reasoning, the Paradox cannot have been caused by coincident trends of any sort. Furthermore, the nonuniform pattern of causality that exists across those countries that do exhibit a causal relationship between the interest rate and the price level is of some interest because it seems reasonable to assume that a strictly bivariate relationship would have produced a uniform pattern. Along the same line, there is a marked change in the nature of the relationship between the French interest rate and price level before and after 1914, even though both periods appear to exhibit the Paradox.[10]

It follows that if neither the interest rate nor the price level is "causing" the other to vary in such a way as to produce the Gibson Paradox, then the observed correlation must be the result of a common relationship with a third variable, or perhaps a set of variables. It appears, then, that an analysis of the Gibson Paradox can be carried out only within the context of a more complete model of the economy, and it is to this problem that the following chapters are addressed. As it turns out, a fairly simple, orthodox model is sufficient to capture the Gibson phenomenon.

---

[10] The correlation between the French interest rate and wholesale price level is .40 for the 1798 to 1914 period and .39 for the 1914 to 1974 period.

APPENDIX TO CHAPTER IV

In Chapter 3, it was shown that large, positive partial correlations between the interest rate and the price level are implied by regressions of a long-term interest rate on an index of wholesale prices and a proxy for the expected rate of change in prices. Moreover, these partial correlations are, in every case, higher than the simple correlations between the same variables. On the other hand, the partial correlations between the interest rate and the price-expectations proxy were found to be uniformly negative. These results were interpreted as contradicting Fisher's explanation of the Gibson Paradox since, if his explanation were correct, not only should the expected rate of change in the price level be positively related to the rate of interest, but the strength of this relationship should be greater than that between the interest rate and the price level.

One might reasonably argue, however, that these results are unfavorable to the Fisher explanation, not because the explanation itself is incorrect, but because price expectations have been modeled incorrectly. Fortunately, one by-product of the time-series models of Chapter 4 is a more satisfactory measure of the expected rate of change of prices, which is calculated by subtracting $\log WPI_t$ from the ARIMA model forecast of $\log WPI_{t+1}$. This measure (denoted π^{**}) is the percentage change in the price level that is expected over the next year if expectations are formed in a "partly rational"[1] manner.

---

[1] See page 63 for a more complete explanation of this term.

Substituting π^{**} for the distributed-lag proxy employed earlier, the equations of Table 3-1 were re-estimated for the countries of Belgium, Canada, France, Germany, Italy, the Netherlands, Switzerland, and the United States. Great Britain, however, has been excluded because an appropriate ARIMA model for an index of British wholesale prices could not be identified. In addition, no estimates are included for the 1798 to 1914 period using French data. The reason for this is that the logarithm of the French wholesale price level appears to have been generated by a random walk process without drift over this period. Consequently, the expected change in log WPI (as measured by π^{**}) is zero throughout. But this means that π^{**} does not appear in the corresponding equation, making it impossible to compare the partial correlations between R and π^{**}, on the one hand, and R and log WPI on the other. Therefore, no meaningful estimates could be made for the 1798 to 1914 period using French data.

Those equations that could be re-estimated are presented in Table 4A-1. As in Table 3-1, the pattern that emerges is one of high, positive partial correlations between the price level and the interest rate and negative partial correlations between the price-expectations proxy and the interest rate. These results lend further support to the argument of Chapter 3 that Fisher's explanation of the Gibson Paradox (as distinguished from his theory of nominal interest rates) is incorrect. If this were not the case, the primary relationship exhibited by regressions of this type would be that between the interest rate and expected price changes, since it is changes in the latter that are alleged to have produced movements in the interest rate that happen to conform with movements in the price level. The fact that this relationship is

TABLE 4A-1

LONG-TERM INTEREST RATE REGRESSED ON THE LOGARITHM OF A WHOLESALE PRICE INDEX
AND A PROXY FOR PRICE EXPECTATIONS (π^{**}), WITH AND WITHOUT LINEAR
TRENDS REMOVED, NINE COUNTRIES, VARIOUS PERIODS, ANNUAL DATA

Country (Period)	Constant	Log of Wholesale Price Index	π^{**}	Time Trend	R^2	D.W.	Partial Correlation Between R and Log(WPI)	Partial Correlation Between R and π^{**}
Belgium (1832–1912)	3.15 (2.73)	.0088 (.68)	−1.00 (.21)		.01	.18	.08	−.02
	5.15 (9.26)	.016 (2.72)	−1.19 (.54)	−.033 (16.55)	.78	.87	.30	−.06
Canada (1900–1973)	2.86 (10.23)	.0099 (6.27)	−3.97 (1.18)		.36	.11	.60	−.14
	7.28 (5.98)	.020 (6.48)	−5.39 (1.73)	−.041 (3.71)	.46	.17	.61	−.20
France (1914–1973)	4.22 (19.28)	.000018 (1.86)	.36 (.26)		.06	.29	.24	.03
	14.09 (7.58)	.00011 (5.79)	.75 (.66)	−.072 (5.33)	.37	.40	.61	.09
Germany (1815–1920)	3.78 (55.64)	.0024 (4.03)	−.20 (.19)		.27	.38	.37	−.02
	3.93 (27.42)	.0024 (4.06)	.0098 (.01)	−.0020 (1.19)	.28	.39	.37	.00

TABLE 4A-1 (continued)

Country (Period)	Constant	Log of Wholesale Price Index	π**	Time Trend	R²	D.W.	Partial Correlation Between R and Log(WPI)	Partial Correlation Between R and π**
Italy (1924–1973)	5.54 (32.99)	.00013 (3.50)	-2.36 (3.79)		.39	.71	.45	-.48
	4.23 (1.55)	.000084 (.83)	-2.43 (3.77)	.0093 (.48)	.39	.73	.12	-.49
Netherlands (1901–1973)	2.83 (14.04)	.0079 (7.73)	-3.17 (1.81)		.46	.19	.68	-.21
	4.10 (3.95)	.0098 (5.32)	-3.30 (1.89)	-.011 (1.25)	.48	.20	.54	-.22
Switzerland (1921–1973)	4.01 (9.26)	-.00058 (.19)	-2.38 (.84)		.02	.23	-.03	-.12
	6.92 (4.00)	.0066 (1.31)	-1.45 (.52)	-.025 (1.73)	.07	.23	.18	-.07
United States (1870–1973)	3.52 (15.41)	.014 (3.52)	-10.82 (2.43)		.13	.11	.33	-.24
	6.60 (15.67)	.047 (9.18)	-9.48 (2.72)	-.038 (8.07)	.47	.13	.68	-.26

Note: 1. t-statistics are in parentheses.
2. π** is the ARIMA model forecast of $\log(WPI_{t+1})$ minus $\log(WPI_t)$. (See Table 4-2 for the ARIMA models used to derive these forecasts.)

Sources: See Data Appendix.

generally not even positive, much less stronger than the relationship between the interest rate and the price level, is inconsistent with the Fisher explanation.

CHAPTER V

A SMALL-SCALE MACROECONOMETRIC MODEL

The principal conclusions deriving from the preceding chapter are first, that the interest rate and the price level are not statistically independent, and second, that the Gibson Paradox is not the product of a strictly bivariate relationship. From these it follows directly that at least one other variable must be causing both R and P to vary in such a manner as to produce a positive correlation between them. It is, therefore, imperative to think of the interest rate and the price level as being endogenous to some macroeconomic model.[1] The immediate objective, then, is to specify and estimate this model. Accordingly, in this chapter a small macroeconomic model that incorporates the interest rate and the price level as endogenous variables is derived from an explicit, and quite orthodox, system of structural equations and is estimated using annual U.S. data. In the following chapter, a relatively new and powerful technique combining econometrics and time series analysis will be used to demonstrate that the model developed here is consistent with information contained in the data. And, finally, this model will be shown to imply a Gibson Paradox-type relationship between the interest rate and the price level.

The following system of structural equations is assumed to characterize the macro economy:

---

[1] This point was made earlier by Sargent (1973a).

$$(5\text{-}1) \quad (y_t^s - k_t) = y[(P_t - {}_tP_{t-1}^e), (y_{t-1}^s - k_{t-1})] \qquad y_1 > 0, y_2 > 0$$

$$(5\text{-}2) \quad e_t = e(y_t, r_t) \qquad e_1 > 0, e_2 < 0$$

$$(5\text{-}3) \quad g_t = G_t/P_t$$

$$(5\text{-}4) \quad y_t^d = e_t + g_t = e(y_t, r_t) + G_t/P_t$$

$$(5\text{-}5) \quad y_t^s = y_t^d = y_t$$

$$(5\text{-}6) \quad m_t^d = L(y_t, R_t) \qquad L_1 > 0, L_2 < 0$$

$$(5\text{-}7) \quad m_t^s = M_t/P_t$$

$$(5\text{-}8) \quad m_t^s = m_t^d = m_t$$

$$(5\text{-}9) \quad R_t = r_t + \pi_t$$

Equation (5-1) is an aggregate supply function of the accelerationist type that has become quite widely accepted in the past few years.[2] A greater than expected increase in the price level[3] causes output supplied (y^s) to be high relative to exogenously-determined, full-employment output (k) because suppliers receive information about the price of their own goods and services faster than they receive information about the aggregate price level (P). Each firm mistakenly believes that the unexpected component of a price rise constitutes an increase in the relative price of its own product. Thus, firms are induced to expand output and to increase their demand for labor, thereby bidding up the nominal wage. And workers, thinking their real wage has risen, are willing to supply the additional labor required to produce this higher level of output. The consequent increase in employment causes the unemployment rate to fall below the natural rate. This "excitement" of real output persists as long as actual prices exceed expected prices.

---

[2] For example, see Gordon (1976) or Hall (1975).

[3] ${}_tP_{t-1}^e$ is the price level expected to prevail in period t as of period t-1.

The same process, but in reverse, operates to depress the supply of output relative to the full-employment level whenever the actual price level falls short of the expected level. This, then, is the theoretical rationale for equation (5-1), which is written in partial-adjustment form to allow for lags in the adjustment of aggregate supply to unexpected changes in prices.[4]

The level of real private expenditure (e), which is the sum of real consumption and investment, is expressed in (5-2) as a function of real income (y) and the real rate of interest (r). In the following equation, (5-3), nominal government purchases of goods and services (G), assumed to be exogenously determined, are deflated by the price level to obtain real government purchases (g). Total real aggregate demand (y^d) is derived in (5-4) by summing private and public demands for output. The equilibrium condition (5-5) ensures equality of aggregate demand and aggregate supply.

Equation (5-6) is a standard liquidity preference function, expressing the demand for real money balances (m^d) as a function of the level of real income (y) and the nominal interest rate (R). The supply of real balances is derived in (5-7) by deflating the nominal money stock (M), which is assumed to be exogenous to the system. Equality between the demand for and supply of real balances is ensured by (5-8).

The final structural equation, (5-9), states that the nominal rate of interest is equal to the real rate plus the expected rate of change in the price level (π). This, of course, is the familiar "Fisher effect." The horizon relevant for the formation of expectations is assumed to be

---

[4]For a more detailed justification of this aggregate supply function, see Lucas (1973).

the interval between periods t and t+1. So π_t is defined as

(5-10) $\quad \pi_t = \log {}_{t+1}P_t^e - \log P_t$,

where $\log {}_{t+1}P_t^e = E(\log P_{t+1})$ as of period t. Defined in this way, π_t is the percentage change in the price level expected between t and t+1. For the moment, the process by which expectations are formed is left unspecified. The following paragraphs detail the derivation of a simple macroeconomic model from this structural system.

Assume, to begin with, that the aggregate supply function, equation (5-1), has the following specification:

(5-11) $\quad (\log y_t^s - \log k_t) = \alpha_o + \alpha_1 (\log P_t - \log {}_t P_{t-1}^e)$
$\qquad + \alpha_2 (\log y_{t-1}^s - \log k_{t-1}).$

After first-differencing, (5-11) becomes

(5-12) $\quad (\Delta \log y_t^s - \Delta \log k_t) = \alpha_1 (\Delta \log P_t - \Delta \log {}_t P_{t-1}^e)$
$\qquad + \alpha_2 (\Delta \log y_{t-1}^s - \Delta \log k_{t-1}).$

Equation (5-12) is the first-difference form of the aggregate supply function and the initial equation of the macro model.

Next, assume that the liquidity preference schedule, equation (5-6), can be written as

(5-13) $\quad \log m_t^d = L'(\log y_t, R_t).$

Since an equivalent expression for equation (5-7) is

(5-14) $\quad \log m_t^s = \log (M_t/P_t),$

equilibrium in the money market requires

(5-15) $\quad \log (M_t/P_t) = L'(\log y_t, R_t).$

Solving (5-15) for R_t yields

(5-16) $R_t = R[\log(M_t/P_t), \log y_t]$.

Then, assuming linearity, (5-16) becomes

(5-17) $R_t = \beta_0 + \beta_1 \log(M_t/P_t) + \beta_2 \log y_t$,

or

(5-18) $R_t = \beta_0 + \beta_1 \log M_t - \beta_1 \log P_t + \beta_2 \log y_t$.

After first differencing, (5-18) becomes

(5-19) $\Delta R_t = \beta_1 \Delta \log M_t - \beta_1 \Delta \log P_t + \beta_2 \Delta \log y_t$,

which constitutes the second equation of the model. This equation, which might be called a portfolio-balance schedule or LM curve, indicates the conditions under which the public will be satisfied with the division of its portfolio between money on the one hand and bonds and equities on the other--assuming, for simplicity, that the public views bonds and equities as perfect substitutes.

The third model equation is derived by solving (5-4) for y_t and expressing the resulting equation in the following general form:

(5-20) $y_t = y(r_t, G_t/P_t)$.

If it is assumed that (5-20) has the following specification:

(5-21) $\log y_t = \delta_0 + \delta_1 r_t + \delta_2 \log(G_t/P_t)$,

then, using (5-9), (5-21) becomes

(5-22) $\log y_t = \delta_0 + \delta_1(R_t - \pi_t) + \delta_2 \log(G_t/P_t)$.

Substituting (5-17) into (5-22) yields a form of the aggregate demand schedule that contains neither R nor r:

(5-23) $\log y_t = \delta_0 + \delta_1[\beta_0 + \beta_1 \log(M_t/P_t) + \beta_2 \log y_t - \pi_t]$
$\qquad + \delta_2 \log(G_t/P_t)$.

Solving for y_t, (5-23) becomes

(5-24) $\log y_t = [(\delta_0 + \delta_1\beta_0)/(1 - \delta_1\beta_2)] + [(\delta_1\beta_1)/(1 - \delta_1\beta_2)] \log (M_t/P_t)$
$+ [\delta_2/(1 - \delta_1\beta_2)] \log (G_t/P_t) - [\delta_1/(1 - \delta_1\beta_2)]\pi_t$

or, more simply,

(5-25) $\log y_t = \gamma_0 + \gamma_1 \log (M_t/P_t) + \gamma_2 \log (G_t/P_t) + \gamma_3 \pi_t$,

which can be expressed equivalently as

(5-26) $\log y_t = \gamma_0 + \gamma_1 \log M_t + \gamma_2 \log G_t - (\gamma_1 + \gamma_2) \log P_t + \gamma_3 \pi_t$.

After first-differencing, (5-26) becomes

(5-27) $\Delta \log y_t = \gamma_1 \Delta \log M_t + \gamma_2 \Delta \log G_t - (\gamma_1 + \gamma_2) \Delta \log P_t + \gamma_3 \Delta \pi$

Equation (5-27) is the first-difference form of the aggregate demand function and the third equation in the model.

Completion of the model requires some assumption regarding the process by which price level expectations are formed. It is shown in the following chapter that the stochastic structure of the first-differenced logarithm of the U.S. price level is that of a first-order autoregressive process with a significantly nonzero constant term. Therefore, the general form of the ARIMA model for $\Delta \log P_t$ is

(5-28) $(1 - \phi^* L) \Delta \log P_t = \theta^* + a_t$,

or

(5-29) $\Delta \log P_t = \theta^* + \phi^* \Delta \log P_{t-1} + a_t$.

Updating (5-29) by one period yields

(5-30) $\Delta \log P_{t+1} = \theta^* + \phi^* \Delta \log P_t + a_{t+1}$,

or, equivalently,

(5-31) $\log P_{t+1} = \theta^* + (1 + \phi^*) \log P_t - \phi^* \log P_{t-1} + a_{t+1}$.

If it is assumed that the public's expectations are "partly rational" in the sense of being consistent with the stochastic process actually generating movements in prices,[5] then the price level (or logarithm thereof) expected in period t+1 will be identical to the one-step ahead ARIMA model forecast of P. Thus, $\log {}_{t+1}P_t^e$ can be expressed as

$$(5\text{-}32) \quad \log {}_{t+1}P_t^e = E[\theta^* + (1 + \phi^*) \log P_t - \phi^* \log P_{t-1} + a_{t+1}]$$
$$= \theta^* + (1 + \phi^*) \log P_t - \phi^* \log P_{t-1}.$$

Substituting (5-32) into (5-10) yields

$$(5\text{-}33) \quad \pi_t = \theta^* + (1 + \phi^*) \log P_t - \phi^* \log P_{t-1} - \log P_t$$

or, more simply,

$$(5\text{-}34) \quad \pi_t = \theta^* + \phi^* \Delta \log P_t.$$

Backdating equation (5-32) by one period and first-differencing yields an expression for $\Delta \log {}_t P_{t-1}^e$ that can be substituted into the aggregate supply function, equation (5-12), to obtain

$$(5\text{-}35)$$
$$(\Delta \log y_t^s - \Delta \log k_t) = \alpha_1[\Delta \log P_t - (1 + \phi^*) \Delta \log P_{t-1} + \phi^* \Delta \log P_{t-2}]$$
$$+ \alpha_2(\Delta \log y_{t-1}^s - \Delta \log k_{t-1})$$
$$= \alpha_1 \Delta \log P_t - \alpha_1(1 + \phi^*) \Delta \log P_{t-1} + \alpha_1\phi^* \Delta \log P_{t-2}$$
$$+ \alpha_2(\Delta \log y_{t-1}^s - \Delta \log k_{t-1}).$$

And the expression for π_t given by (5-34) can be substituted into the aggregate demand function, equation (5-27), to yield

$$(5\text{-}36) \quad \Delta \log y_t = \gamma_1 \Delta \log M_t + \gamma_2 \Delta \log G_t - (\gamma_1 + \gamma_2) \Delta \log P_t$$
$$+ \gamma_3 \Delta(\theta^* + \phi^* \Delta \log P_t)$$
$$= \gamma_1 \Delta \log M_t + \gamma_2 \Delta \log G_t + (\gamma_3\phi^* - \gamma_1 - \gamma_2) \Delta \log P_t$$
$$- \gamma_3\phi^* \Delta \log P_{t-1}.$$

---

[5] This procedure for modeling expectations is supported to a considerable degree by the work of Feige and Pearce (1976).

This completes the derivation of the macro model, which consists of equations (5-35), (5-36), and (5-19). Variables endogenous to the model are $\Delta \log y_t$, $\Delta \log P_t$, and ΔR_t. The exogenous variables are $\Delta \log M_t$, $\Delta \log G_t$, and $\Delta \log k_t$. For convenience, the entire model is summarized below:

Aggregate Supply Schedule

(5-35) $(\Delta \log y_t^S - \Delta \log k_t) = \alpha_1 \Delta \log P_t - \alpha_1(1 + \phi^*) \Delta \log P_{t-1}$
$\qquad + \alpha_1 \phi^* \Delta \log P_{t-2} + \alpha_2 (\Delta \log y_{t-1}^S - \Delta \log k_{t-1})$

Aggregate Demand Schedule

(5-36) $\Delta \log y_t = \gamma_1 \Delta \log M_t + \gamma_2 \Delta \log G_t + (\gamma_3 \phi^* - \gamma_1 - \gamma_2) \Delta \log P_t$
$\qquad - \gamma_3 \phi^* \Delta \log P_{t-1}$

Portfolio Balance Schedule

(5-19) $\Delta R_t = \beta_1 \Delta \log M_t - \beta_1 \Delta \log P_t + \beta_2 \Delta \log y_t.$

The model equations were estimated using three-stage least squares and annual U.S. data for the period from 1890 to 1969.[6] Gross national product in billions of 1958 dollars was used to measure real income (y), while the price level (P) is the corresponding implicit GNP deflator. The interest rate (R) from 1890 to 1899 is Macaulay's adjusted index of American railroad bond yields plus 12 basis points, and from 1900 to 1969 it is Durand's basic yield on 30-year corporate bonds.[7] The concept of the money stock (M) employed here is broadly-defined money, or M2, consisting of currency held by the public plus

---

[6] Data sources and actual numbers used in estimating the model are contained in the Data Appendix.

[7] Twelve basis points were added to Macaulay's railroad bond yields in order to splice that series with Durand's corporate bond yields. The latter exceeded the former by that amount in 1900.

demand and time deposits in commercial banks.[8] And federal, state, and local government purchases of goods and services (G) were used as a measure of aggregate demand originating in the public sector. Both M and G are in current dollars. Finally, an index of full-employment output (k) was constructed in the following manner:

$$(5\text{-}39) \quad k_t = K_t^{w_K} \cdot L_t^{w_L},$$

where K and L are indexes of total capital and the civilian labor force,[9] respectively, and w_K and w_L are the relative factor shares of capital and labor.

The reasoning behind equation (5-39) is straightforward. Assume that the aggregate production function has the following Cobb-Douglas specification:

$$(5\text{-}40) \quad k_t = A(t) \, K_t^{w_K} \cdot L_t^{w_L},$$

where K, L, w_K, and w_L are as described above, and A(t) represents neutral technical change. Taking logarithms of each side of (5-40) and first-differencing yields

$$(5\text{-}41) \quad \Delta \log k_t = \Delta \log A(t) + w_K \Delta \log K_t + w_L \Delta \log L_t.$$

Substituting (5-41) into equation (5-35), the aggregate supply function, and moving $\Delta \log A(t)$ to the right-hand side gives[10]

---

[8] Statistics on narrowly-defined money, or M2 less time deposits, do not exist for the entire 1890 to 1969 period because no distinction between demand and time deposits was made prior to 1915. For a discussion of this point, see Friedman and Schwartz (1963).

[9] These indexes are fully described in the Data Appendix.

[10] For purposes of clarity, the lagged dependent variable appearing in (5-35) has been omitted.

(5-42) $[\Delta \log y_t^s - (w_K \Delta \log K_t + w_L \Delta \log L_t)] = \Delta \log A(t)$
$+ \alpha_1 \Delta \log P_t - \alpha_1 (1 + \phi^*) \Delta \log P_{t-1} + \alpha_1 \phi^* \Delta \log P_{t-2}.$

Equation (5-42) can be estimated using $w_K \Delta \log K_t + w_L \Delta \log L_t$ as a proxy for $\Delta \log k_t$ so long as $\Delta \log A(t)$ is relatively stable and a constant term is included to capture the average rate of technical change.

In constructing this index of full-employment output, w_K and w_L were set equal to .35 and .65, respectively. These numbers are very close to the estimates obtained by Solow (1957) for the period from 1909 to 1949. Nonetheless, k appears to be almost totally insensitive to the choice of values for w_K and w_L, as is demonstrated by the following correlation matrix in which $\log k_1 = .25 \log K + .75 \log L$, $\log k_2 = .35 \log K + .65 \log L$, and $\log k_3 = .50 \log K + .50 \log L$:

Correlations Between $\log k_1$, $\log k_2$, and $\log k_3$

	$\log k_1$	$\log k_2$	$\log k_3$
$\log k_1$	1.0000		
$\log k_2$	.9998	1.0000	
$\log k_3$	.9986	.9995	1.0000

These figures clearly indicate that the decision to use .35 and .65 as relative factor shares is not one that can be expected to influence the outcome in any significant way.

As indicated above, the model was estimated using three-stage least squares. All restrictions on the coefficients implicit in the model equations were imposed. Furthermore, a constant term was added in estimating all three equations even though strong theoretical grounds exist for doing so only in the case of the aggregate supply function. Estimated equations and relevant summary statistics are presented in Table 5-1.

Excluding constant terms, seven of the eleven coefficients have the expected sign and are significant at the 5% level. Of the other four, only the coefficient on $\Delta \log y_t$ in the portfolio balance schedule has the wrong sign, and it is insignificantly different from zero. Evidence regarding the speed of adjustment of real income to unexpected changes in the price level is ambiguous, as the t-score for the coefficient on the lagged dependent variable is close to, but does not exceed, the critical value for a t-statistic at the 5% level of significance. This variable, however, was retained in the final estimation. None of the coefficients of determination (R^2) is particularly high, but this is a fairly common characteristic of first-differenced equations. Nonetheless, the small, negative R^2 associated with the estimate of the aggregate supply function is disturbing.

These reservations notwithstanding, the estimates presented in Table 5-1 are modestly impressive. Furthermore, the significance of those variables entering the model by way of the assumed expectations-formation mechanism lends support to the "partly rational" approach employed here. Even at this stage, the model appears to be a reasonable framework for an examination of the relationship between the interest rate and the price level. This impression is significantly reinforced in the following chapter in which the model passes a more rigorous test of its adequacy.

TABLE 5-1

THREE-STAGE LEAST SQUARES ESTIMATES OF THE MODEL EQUATIONS

Aggregate Supply Schedule

(5-35) $(\Delta \log y_t - \Delta \log k_t) = .0097 + .75^{**} \Delta \log P_t - .70^{**} \Delta \log P_{t-1}$
$\qquad\qquad\qquad\qquad\quad\;\;(.35)\quad\;(3.62)\qquad\qquad\quad\;(3.43)$

$\qquad\qquad\qquad - .058 \Delta \log P_{t-2} + .16(\Delta \log y_{t-1} - \Delta \log k_{t-1})$
$\qquad\qquad\qquad\;\;(.42)\qquad\qquad\quad\;(1.48)$

$R^2 = -.04 \qquad D.F. = 73 \qquad D.W. = 1.96 \qquad \hat{\sigma}^2 = .00484$

Aggregate Demand Schedule

(5-36) $\Delta \log y_t = .0087 + .48^{**} \Delta \log M_t + .092^{**} \Delta \log G_t$
$\qquad\qquad\qquad(1.25)\quad(3.81)\qquad\qquad\;(5.05)$

$\qquad\qquad + .075 \Delta \log P_t - .64^{**} \Delta \log P_{t-1}$
$\qquad\qquad\;\;(.37)\qquad\qquad(5.20)$

$R^2 = .51 \qquad D.F. = 73 \qquad D.W. = 1.90 \qquad \hat{\sigma}^2 = .00210$

Portfolio Balance Schedule

(5-19) $\Delta R_t = .0011^{**} - .020^{*} \Delta \log M_t + .020^{*} \Delta \log P_t - .0015 \Delta \log y_t$
$\qquad\qquad\;\;(2.69)\quad\;(2.16)\qquad\qquad\;(2.16)\qquad\qquad\;(.22)$

$R^2 = .09 \qquad D.F. = 74 \qquad D.W. = 1.67 \qquad \hat{\sigma}^2 = .00000669$

Note: 1. t-statistics are in parentheses.
2. * indicates significance at the 5% level (one-tail test).
   ** indicates significance at the 1% level (one-tail test).

CHAPTER VI

TIME SERIES ANALYSIS AND ECONOMETRIC MODEL CONSTRUCTION:
AN APPLICATION AND AN EXTENSION

Zellner (1975) and Zellner and Palm (1974, 1975) have demonstrated that if the variables appearing in a linear dynamic econometric model can be represented by a multivariate autoregressive integrated moving average process, then it is possible to solve for the stochastic processes generating individual endogenous variables. Furthermore, these processes, referred to as final equations (FE's), are in ARIMA form, so they may be checked against direct estimates of the ARIMA processes characterizing the endogenous variables. If the model implications are consistent with this information contained in the data, then confidence in the model is greatly enhanced. If not, the model must be revised. In what follows, this technique is applied to the macro model developed in the preceding chapter. It is shown that the model does, in fact, imply stochastic processes for $\Delta \log y$, $\Delta \log P$, and ΔR that are consistent with those obtained by direct estimation. And, more importantly, the analysis is found to have immediate implications for the Gibson Paradox.

Rewriting the aggregate supply schedule with endogenous variables on the left-hand side and exogenous variables on the right yields[1]

---

[1] To simplify the algebraic manipulations, constant terms have been omitted throughout. The results are unaffected.

(6-1) $\Delta \log y_t - \alpha_2 \Delta \log y_{t-1} - \alpha_1 \Delta \log P_t + \alpha_1(1 + \phi^*) \Delta \log P_{t-1}$
$- \alpha_1 \phi^* \Delta \log P_{t-2} = \Delta \log k_t - \alpha_2 \Delta \log k_{t-1}.$

Then, substituting lag polynomials for the coefficients on current and lagged values of each variable, (6-1) becomes

(6-2) $h_{11}(L) \Delta \log y_t + h_{12}(L) \Delta \log P_t + h_{13}(L) \Delta R_t = h_{14}(L) \Delta \log M_t$
$+ h_{15}(L) \Delta \log G_t + h_{16}(L) \Delta \log k_t,$

where $h_{11}(L) = 1 - \alpha_2 L$ $\qquad h_{14}(L) = 0$
$h_{12}(L) = -\alpha_1 + \alpha_1(1 + \phi^*)L - \alpha_1 \phi^* L^2 \qquad h_{15}(L) = 0$
$h_{13}(L) = 0 \qquad h_{16}(L) = 1 - \alpha_2 L.$

Similarly, the aggregate demand schedule can be rewritten as

(6-3) $\Delta \log y_t + (\gamma_1 + \gamma_2 - \gamma_3 \phi^*) \Delta \log P_t + \gamma_3 \phi^* \Delta \log P_{t-1} = \gamma_1 \Delta \log M_t$
$+ \gamma_2 \Delta \log G_t$

or

(6-4) $h_{21}(L) \Delta \log y_t + h_{22}(L) \Delta \log P_t + h_{23}(L) \Delta R_t = h_{24}(L) \Delta \log M_t$
$+ h_{25}(L) \Delta \log G_t + h_{26}(L) \Delta \log k_t,$

where $h_{21}(L) = 1 \qquad h_{24}(L) = \gamma_1$
$h_{22}(L) = (\gamma_1 + \gamma_2 - \gamma_3 \phi^*) + \gamma_3 \phi^* L \qquad h_{25}(L) = \gamma_2$
$h_{23}(L) = 0 \qquad h_{26}(L) = 0.$

And the portfolio balance schedule can be rewritten as

(6-5) $-\beta_2 \Delta \log y_t + \beta_1 \Delta \log P_t + \Delta R_t = \beta_1 \Delta \log M_t$

or

(6-6) $h_{31}(L) \Delta \log y_t + h_{32}(L) \Delta \log P_t + h_{33}(L) \Delta R_t = h_{34}(L) \Delta \log M_t$
$+ h_{35}(L) \Delta \log G_t + h_{36}(L) \Delta \log k_t,$

where $h_{31}(L) = -\beta_2$ $\quad\quad h_{34}(L) = \beta_1$
$h_{32}(L) = \beta_1$ $\quad\quad h_{35}(L) = 0$
$h_{33}(L) = 1$ $\quad\quad h_{36}(L) = 0.$

Let u_{1t}, u_{2t}, and u_{3t} be white-noise disturbance terms in the aggregate supply, aggregate demand, and portfolio balance schedules, respectively. Then, substituting in for those $h_{ij}(L)$'s known to be either zero or one, the model can be written in matrix form as

$$(6\text{-}7) \begin{bmatrix} h_{11} & h_{12} & 0 \\ 1 & h_{22} & 0 \\ h_{31} & h_{32} & 1 \end{bmatrix} \begin{bmatrix} \Delta \log y_t \\ \Delta \log P_t \\ \Delta R_t \end{bmatrix} = \begin{bmatrix} 0 & 0 & h_{16} \\ h_{24} & h_{25} & 0 \\ h_{34} & 0 & 0 \end{bmatrix} \begin{bmatrix} \Delta \log M_t \\ \Delta \log G_t \\ \Delta \log k_t \end{bmatrix} + \begin{bmatrix} u_{1t} \\ u_{2t} \\ u_{3t} \end{bmatrix},$$

where, for simplicity, $h_{ij}(L) = h_{ij}$. Let H denote the matrix of h_{ij}'s premultiplying the column vector of endogenous variables in equation (6-7). The determinant [det(H)], cofactor matrix (C), and adjoint matrix (C^T) of H are

$$(6\text{-}8) \quad \det(H) = \det \begin{bmatrix} h_{11} & h_{12} \\ 1 & h_{22} \end{bmatrix} = h_{11}h_{22} - h_{12},$$

$$(6\text{-}9) \quad C = \begin{bmatrix} h_{22} & -1 & h_{32}-h_{22}h_{31} \\ -h_{12} & h_{11} & h_{12}h_{31}-h_{11}h_{32} \\ 0 & 0 & h_{11}h_{22}-h_{12} \end{bmatrix},$$

and

$$(6\text{-}10) \quad C^T = \begin{bmatrix} h_{22} & -h_{12} & 0 \\ -1 & h_{11} & 0 \\ h_{32}-h_{22}h_{31} & h_{12}h_{31}-h_{11}h_{32} & h_{11}h_{22}-h_{12} \end{bmatrix}.$$

Since $C^T H = \det(H)$, premultiplying equation (6-7) by C^T yields

$$(6\text{-}11) \quad (h_{11}h_{22}-h_{12}) \begin{bmatrix} \Delta \log y_t \\ \Delta \log P_t \\ \Delta R_t \end{bmatrix} = C^T \begin{bmatrix} 0 & 0 & h_{16} \\ h_{24} & h_{25} & 0 \\ h_{34} & 0 & 0 \end{bmatrix} \begin{bmatrix} \Delta \log M_t \\ \Delta \log G_t \\ \Delta \log k_t \end{bmatrix} + C^T \begin{bmatrix} u_{1t} \\ u_{2t} \\ u_{3t} \end{bmatrix}.$$

The equations described by (6-11) are the so-called Transfer Functions (TF's), each of which expresses one endogenous variable in terms of its own lagged values, current and lagged values of the exogenous variables, and a composite, moving-average disturbance term. Although important differences exist, the TF's are similar in appearance and usefulness to the more conventional reduced-form equations.[2] Finally, since

(6-12)

$$C^T \begin{bmatrix} 0 & 0 & h_{16} \\ h_{24} & h_{25} & 0 \\ h_{34} & 0 & 0 \end{bmatrix} = \begin{bmatrix} -h_{12}h_{24} & -h_{12}h_{25} & h_{22}h_{16} \\ h_{11}h_{24} & h_{11}h_{25} & -h_{16} \\ h_{24}(h_{12}h_{31}-h_{11}h_{32}) & h_{25}(h_{12}h_{31}-h_{11}h_{32}) & h_{16}(h_{32}-h_{22}h_{31}) \\ +h_{34}(h_{11}h_{22}-h_{12}) & & \end{bmatrix}$$

and

$$(6\text{-}13) \quad C^T \begin{bmatrix} u_{1t} \\ u_{2t} \\ u_{3t} \end{bmatrix} = \begin{bmatrix} h_{22}u_{1t} & -h_{12}u_{2t} \\ -u_{1t} & +h_{11}u_{2t} \\ (h_{32}-h_{22}h_{31})u_{1t}+(h_{12}h_{31}-h_{11}h_{32})u_{2t}+(h_{11}h_{22}-h_{12})u_{3t} \end{bmatrix},$$

---

[2] See Zellner and Palm (1974).

the implied Transfer Functions for $\Delta \log y$, $\Delta \log P$, and ΔR can be written as

$$(6\text{-}14) \quad (h_{11}h_{22}-h_{12}) \Delta \log y_t = -(h_{12}h_{24}) \Delta \log M_t - (h_{12}h_{25}) \Delta \log G_t$$
$$+ (h_{22}h_{16}) \Delta \log k_t + (h_{22})u_{1t} - (h_{12})u_{2t} ,$$

$$(6\text{-}15) \quad (h_{11}h_{22}-h_{12}) \Delta \log P_t = (h_{11}h_{24}) \Delta \log M_t + (h_{11}h_{25}) \Delta \log G_t$$
$$- (h_{16}) \Delta \log k_t - u_{1t} + (h_{11})u_{2t} ,$$

and

$$(6\text{-}16) \quad (h_{11}h_{22}-h_{12}) \Delta R_t = [h_{24}(h_{12}h_{31}-h_{11}h_{32}) + h_{34}(h_{11}h_{22}-h_{12})] \Delta \log M_t$$
$$+ [h_{25}(h_{12}h_{31}-h_{11}h_{32})] \Delta \log G_t + [h_{16}(h_{32}-h_{22}h_{31})] \Delta \log k_t$$
$$+ (h_{32}-h_{22}h_{31})u_{1t} + (h_{12}h_{31}-h_{11}h_{32})u_{2t} + (h_{11}h_{22}-h_{12})u_{3t} ,$$

respectively.

General expressions for the ARIMA processes generating the exogenous variables are as follows:

$$(6\text{-}17) \quad \phi_1(L) \Delta \log M_t = \theta_1(L)a_{Mt},$$

$$(6\text{-}18) \quad \phi_2(L) \Delta \log G_t = \theta_2(L)a_{Gt},$$

and

$$(6\text{-}19) \quad \phi_3(L) \Delta \log k_t = \theta_3(L)a_{kt},$$

where the $\phi_i(L)$'s and the $\theta_i(L)$'s are finite lag polynomials, and the a_t's are white noise processes. Since $\phi_1(L)$, $\phi_2(L)$, and $\phi_3(L)$ are invertible, equations (6-17), (6-18), and (6-19) can be rewritten as

$$(6\text{-}20) \quad \Delta \log M_t = \phi_1(L)^{-1}\theta_1(L)a_{Mt},$$

$$(6\text{-}21) \quad \Delta \log G_t = \phi_2(L)^{-1}\theta_2(L)a_{Gt},$$

and

(6-22) $\Delta \log k_t = \phi_3(L)^{-1}\theta_3(L)a_{kt}.$

After suppressing (L) to simplify the notation, these become

(6-23) $\Delta \log M_t = \phi_1^{-1}\theta_1 a_{Mt},$

(6-24) $\Delta \log G_t = \phi_2^{-1}\theta_2 a_{Gt},$

and

(6-25) $\Delta \log k_t = \phi_3^{-1}\theta_3 a_{kt}.$

Substituting (6-23), (6-24), and (6-25) into the Transfer Function for $\Delta \log y$, equation (6-14), yields the implied Final Equation (FE) for $\Delta \log y$, which is

(6-26) $(h_{11}h_{22}-h_{12})\Delta \log y_t = -(h_{12}h_{24})\phi_1^{-1}\theta_1 a_{Mt} - (h_{12}h_{25})\phi_2^{-1}\theta_2 a_{Gt}$
$+ (h_{22}h_{16})\phi_3^{-1}\theta_3 a_{kt} + (h_{22})u_{1t} - (h_{12})u_{2t}$

or, multiplying through by ϕ_1, ϕ_2, and ϕ_3,

(6-27) $\phi_1\phi_2\phi_3(h_{11}h_{22}-h_{12})\Delta \log y_t = -\phi_2\phi_3(h_{12}h_{24})\theta_1 a_{Mt} - \phi_1\phi_3(h_{12}h_{25})\theta_2 a_{Gt}$
$+ \phi_1\phi_2(h_{22}h_{16})\theta_3 a_{kt} + \phi_1\phi_2\phi_3(h_{22})u_{1t} - \phi_1\phi_2\phi_3(h_{12})u_{2t}.$

Similarly, the implied Final Equation for $\Delta \log P$ is

(6-28) $(h_{11}h_{22}-h_{12})\Delta \log P_t = (h_{11}h_{24})\phi_1^{-1}\theta_1 a_{Mt} + (h_{11}h_{25})\phi_2^{-1}\theta_2 a_{Gt}$
$- (h_{16})\phi_3^{-1}\theta_3 a_{kt} - u_{1t} + (h_{11})u_{2t}$

or

(6-29) $\phi_1\phi_2\phi_3(h_{11}h_{22}-h_{12})\Delta \log P_t = \phi_2\phi_3(h_{11}h_{24})\theta_1 a_{Mt} + \phi_1\phi_3(h_{11}h_{25})\theta_2 a_{Gt}$
$- \phi_1\phi_2(h_{16})\theta_3 a_{kt} - \phi_1\phi_2\phi_3 u_{1t} + \phi_1\phi_2\phi_3(h_{11})u_{2t},$

and the implied Final Equation for ΔR is

(6-30) $(h_{11}h_{22}-h_{12})\Delta R_t = [h_{24}(h_{12}h_{31}-h_{11}h_{32}) + h_{34}(h_{11}h_{22}-h_{12})]\phi_1^{-1}\theta_1 a_{Mt}$
$+ [h_{25}(h_{12}h_{31}-h_{11}h_{32})]\phi_2^{-1}\theta_2 a_{Gt}$
$+ [h_{16}(h_{32}-h_{22}h_{31})]\phi_3^{-1}\theta_3 a_{kt} + (h_{32}-h_{22}h_{31})u_{1t}$
$+ (h_{12}h_{31}-h_{11}h_{32})u_{2t} + (h_{11}h_{22}-h_{12})u_{3t}$

or

(6-31) $\phi_1\phi_2\phi_3(h_{11}h_{22}-h_{12})\Delta R_t = \phi_2\phi_3[h_{24}(h_{12}h_{31}-h_{11}h_{32})$
$+ h_{34}(h_{11}h_{22}-h_{12})]\theta_1 a_{Mt} + \phi_1\phi_3[h_{25}(h_{12}h_{31}-h_{11}h_{32})]\theta_2 a_{Gt}$
$+ \phi_1\phi_2[h_{16}(h_{32}-h_{22}h_{31})]\theta_3 a_{kt} + \phi_1\phi_2\phi_3(h_{32}-h_{22}h_{31})u_{1t}$
$+ \phi_1\phi_2\phi_3(h_{12}h_{31}-h_{11}h_{32})u_{2t} + \phi_1\phi_2\phi_3(h_{11}h_{22}-h_{12})u_{3t}$.

Equations (6-27), (6-29), and (6-31) express the endogenous variables in ARIMA form as functions of the autoregressive and moving-average lag polynomials in the processes generating the exogenous variables (the ϕ_i's and the θ_i's, respectively), the model parameters (via the h_{ij}'s), the innovations in the processes generating the exogenous variables (the a_t's), and the disturbances in the model equations (the u_{it}'s). Moreover, the FE's described by these equations are testable implications of the model since they can be checked against direct estimates of the ARIMA forms of the endogenous variables. If these checks reveal substantial dissimilarities between actual and implied FE's, then it is likely that the model is deficient in some respect and should be revised. If, on the other hand, the implied FE's are sufficiently similar to the direct ARIMA estimates, then confidence in the model is enhanced.

In order to carry out this test of model adequacy, it was necessary to quantify the implied FE's by substituting estimates of the ϕ_i's, the θ_i's, and the h_{ij}'s into equations (6-27), (6-29), and (6-31).

Since the ϕ_i's and the θ_i's are parts of the ARIMA processes generating the exogenous variables, the techniques of Box and Jenkins (1970) were used to estimate univariate ARIMA models for log M, log G, and log k. Fitted models are shown in Table 6-1.[3] As can be seen, over the 1890 to 1969 period, log M, log G, and log k appear to have been generated by ARIMA (1,1,1), (0,1,1), and (1,1,0) processes, respectively. Estimates of the ϕ_i's and the θ_i's implicit in these fitted models are as follows:

$$\hat{\phi}_1 = 1 - .38L \qquad \hat{\theta}_1 = 1 + .38L$$
$$\hat{\phi}_2 = 1 \qquad \hat{\theta}_2 = 1 + .45L$$
$$\hat{\phi}_3 = 1 - .57L \qquad \hat{\theta}_3 = 1.$$

Furthermore, the h_{ij}'s not equal to zero or one were defined in terms of the model parameters as follows:

$$h_{11} = 1 - \alpha_2 L \qquad h_{25} = \gamma_2$$
$$h_{12} = -\alpha_1 + \alpha_1(1 + \phi^*)L - \alpha_1 \phi^* L^2 \qquad h_{31} = -\beta_2$$
$$h_{16} = 1 - \alpha_2 L \qquad h_{32} = \beta_1$$
$$h_{22} = (\gamma_1 + \gamma_2 - \gamma_3 \phi^*) + \gamma_3 \phi^* L \qquad h_{34} = \beta_1.$$
$$h_{24} = \gamma_1$$

Substituting estimated values of the model parameters into these expressions and then setting those parameters not significantly different from zero equal precisely to zero yields:

---

[3] To ensure comparability with the estimated macro model, both the data and sample period are as described in the previous chapter. Plots of estimated autocorrelation and partial autocorrelation functions for each variable appear in Appendix B. Estimates of competing, but inferior, ARIMA models--including relevant overfits--are in Appendix C.

TABLE 6-1

ARIMA MODELS FITTED TO THE LOGARITHM OF THE NOMINAL MONEY STOCK,
THE LOGARITHM OF NOMINAL GOVERNMENT PURCHASES OF GOODS AND SERVICES,
AND THE LOGARITHM OF AN INDEX OF FULL-EMPLOYMENT OUTPUT,
UNITED STATES, 1890 TO 1969, ANNUAL DATA

Variable: Logarithm of the Nominal Money Stock (Log M)
Time Series Process: ARIMA (1,1,1)
Fitted Model:

$$(1 - .38L) \Delta \log M_t = .036 + (1 + .38L)\hat{a}_{Mt}$$
$$(2.41) \qquad\qquad (3.01) \quad (2.41)$$

$R^2 = .40$

D.F. = 76

$\hat{\sigma}^2 = .00244$

Box-Pierce Statistics	Degrees of Freedom	Critical Q Values (10% level of sig.)
Q(12) = 4.7	10	16.0
Q(24) = 15.7	22	30.8

Variable: Logarithm of Nominal Government Purchases of Goods and Services (Log G)
Time Series Process: ARIMA (0,1,1)
Fitted Model:

$$\Delta \log G_t = .073 + (1 + .45L)\hat{a}_{Gt}$$
$$(1.89) \quad (4.39)$$

$R^2 = .13$

D.F. = 77

$\hat{\sigma}^2 = .0562$

Box-Pierce Statistics	Degrees of Freedom	Critical Q Values (10% level of sig.)
Q(12) = 9.5	11	17.3
Q(24) = 15.7	23	32.0

Variable: Logarithm of an Index of Full-Employment Output (Log k)
Time Series Process: ARIMA (1,1,0)
Fitted Model:

$$(1 - .57L) \Delta \log k_t = .0086 + \hat{a}_{kt}$$
$$(6.06) \qquad\qquad (4.02)$$

$R^2 = .31$

D.F. = 77

$\hat{\sigma}^2 = .0000980$

Box-Pierce Statistics	Degrees of Freedom	Critical Q Values (10% level of sig.)
Q(12) = 11.2	11	17.3
Q(24) = 16.7	23	32.0

Note:
1. t-statistics are in parentheses.
2. L is a lag operator such that $L^n x_t = x_{t-n}$.
3. Q(K) is distributed χ^2 with K - p - q degrees of freedom, where p + q equals the number of autoregressive and moving average parameters estimated.

Sources: See Data Appendix.

$$\hat{h}_{11} = 1 - .16L \approx 1$$
$$\hat{h}_{12} = -.75 + .70L + .058L^2 \approx -.75 + .70L$$
$$\hat{h}_{16} = 1 - .16L \approx 1$$
$$\hat{h}_{22} = -.075 + .64L \approx .64L$$
$$\hat{h}_{24} = .48$$
$$\hat{h}_{25} = .092$$
$$\hat{h}_{31} = .0015 \approx 0$$
$$\hat{h}_{32} = -.020$$
$$\hat{h}_{34} = -.020.$$

Finally, substituting the $\hat{\phi}_i$'s, the $\hat{\theta}_i$'s, and the $\hat{h}_{ij}$'s into equations (6-27), (6-29), and (6-31) gives the following estimates of the implied FE's:

(6-32) $(1 - .38L)(1 - .57L)(.75 - .06L) \Delta \log y_t =$
$\quad - (1 - .57L)(-.36 + .34L)(1 + .38L)a_{Mt}$
$\quad - (1 - .38L)(1 - .57L)(-.069 + .064L)(1 + .45L)a_{Gt}$
$\quad + (1 - .38L)(.64L)a_{kt} + (1 - .38L)(1 - .57L)(.64L)u_{1t}$
$\quad - (1 - .38L)(1 - .57L)(-.75 + .70L)u_{2t},$

(6-33) $(1 - .38L)(1 - .57L)(.75 - .06L) \Delta \log P_t =$
$\quad (1 - .57L)(.48)(1 + .38L)a_{Mt}$
$\quad + (1 - .38L)(1 - .57L)(.092)(1 + .45L)a_{Gt}$
$\quad - (1 - .38L)a_{kt} - (1 - .38L)(1 - .57L)u_{1t}$
$\quad + (1 - .38L)(1 - .57L)u_{2t},$

and

(6-34) $(1 - .38L)(1 - .57L)(.75 - .06L) \Delta R_t =$
$\quad (1 - .57L)(-.0054 + .0012L)(1 + .45L)a_{Mt}$
$\quad + (1 - .38L)(1 - .57L)(.0018)(1 + .45L)a_{Gt}$
$\quad + (1 - .38L)(-.020)a_{kt} + (1 - .38L)(1 - .57L)(-.020)u_{1t}$
$\quad + (1 - .38L)(1 - .57L)(.020)u_{2t}$
$\quad + (1 - .38L)(1 - .57L)(.75 - .06L)u_{3t}.$

These results suggest that, if the model is correct, log y, log P, and R should appear to have been generated by ARIMA (3,1,4), (3,1,3), and (3,1,3) processes, respectively.[4] To test the adequacy of the model by these implications, the techniques of Box and Jenkins were used to fit ARIMA models directly to the data.[5] As Table 6-2 indicates, the stochastic structure of the first difference of log P is that of a first-order autoregressive process, while log y and R appear to have been generated by random walk processes.[6] Thus, the autoregressive and moving-average parts of the FE's estimated directly from the data are of a much lower order than are those implied by the model.

On the face of it, the implications of the model are inconsistent with information contained in the data, suggesting that the model ought to be revised. However, such a conclusion would be premature for the following reason. Except when applied to the simplest of econometric models, the Zellner-Palm procedure frequently leads to implied FE's having high-order autoregressive and moving-average parts. Yet empirical evidence indicates that many, if not most, economic time

---

[4] The degree of the autoregressive part of each implied FE is determined by the highest power of L appearing on the left-hand side of the equation. Similarly, the degree of the moving-average part is determined by the highest power of L in any of the terms on the right-hand side of each FE.

[5] Footnote 3 on page 76 applies here also.

[6] A time series variable Z_t is said to have been generated by a random walk process if its first difference is white noise--that is, if its ARIMA representation is $\Delta Z_t = a_t$. If Z_t also exhibits a deterministic trend, then its ARIMA representation is $\Delta Z_t = a_0 + a_t$, and Z_t is said to have been generated by a random walk process with drift. In the present context, log y is a realization of a random walk process with drift (because the constant term in its estimated ARIMA model is significantly non-zero), and R is a realization of a simple random walk process.

TABLE 6-2

ARIMA MODELS FITTED TO THE LOGARITHM OF REAL GROSS NATIONAL PRODUCT,
THE LOGARITHM OF THE IMPLICIT GNP DEFLATOR,
AND THE LONG-TERM INTEREST RATE,
UNITED STATES, 1890 TO 1969, ANNUAL DATA

Variable: Logarithm of Real Gross National Product (Log y)
Time Series Process: ARIMA (0,1,0)
Fitted Model:

$$\Delta \log y_t = \underset{(4.56)}{.0072} + \hat{a}_{yt}$$

D.F. = 78
$\hat{\sigma}^2$ = .00407

Box-Pierce Statistics	Degrees of Freedom	Critical Q Values (10% level of sig.)
Q(12) = 14.8	12	18.5
Q(24) = 20.8	24	33.2

Variable: Logarithm of the Implicit GNP Deflator (Log P)
Time Series Process: ARIMA (1,1,0)
Fitted Model:

$$(1 - \underset{(4.19)}{.43L}) \Delta \log P_t = \underset{(2.03)}{.012} + \hat{a}_{Pt}$$

R^2 = .18
D.F. = 77
$\hat{\sigma}^2$ = .00228

Box-Pierce Statistics	Degrees of Freedom	Critical Q Values (10% level of sig.)
Q(12) = 4.4	11	17.3
Q(24) = 17.9	23	32.0

Variable: Long-Term Interest Rate (R)
Time Series Process: ARIMA (0,1,0)
Fitted Model:

$$\Delta R_t = \underset{(1.17)}{.00035} + \hat{a}_{Rt}$$

D.F. = 78
$\hat{\sigma}^2$ = .00000702

Box-Pierce Statistics	Degrees of Freedom	Critical Q Values (10% level of sig.)
Q(12) = 15.4	12	18.5
Q(24) = 22.1	24	33.2

Note: 1. t-statistics are in parentheses.
2. L is a lag operator such that $L^n x_t = x_{t-n}$.
3. Q(K) is distributed χ^2 with K - p - q degrees of freedom, where p + q equals the number of autoregressive and moving average parameters estimated.

Sources: See Data Appendix.

series variables are adequately described by ARIMA processes of a very low order. Indeed, it is rarely necessary to fit a model more complex than an ARIMA (1,1,1). In an effort to reconcile these seemingly inconsistent observations, an extension of the Zellner-Palm procedure is developed below. This analysis reveals that the model implications are considerably more accurate than appears to be the case at first glance.

In extending the work of Zellner and Palm, it seems worthwhile to consider the possibility that the moving-average parts of the implied FE's are dominated by one or more of the constituent moving-average terms. If this is the case and if the model is correct, then the moving-average parts of the FE's estimated directly from the data should most closely resemble the dominant moving-average terms in the implied FE's. It follows that the valid comparison for purposes of assessing model adequacy would not be between actual FE's and implied FE's in which all of the moving average terms appear, but between actual FE's and implied FE's modified to include only the dominant moving-average terms. The difficulty, of course, lies in establishing a criterion for dominance and in determining which, if any, of the moving-average terms in the implied FE's satisfy this criterion.

It would be possible to use estimates of the variance of the a_t's and the u_t's (from Tables 6-1 and 5-1, respectively) to derive an estimate of the variance of each of the moving-average terms in the implied FE's. The dominant terms would then be those with the largest estimated variances. Unfortunately, this criterion is deficient in that any subsequent cancellation of a common factor from both sides of an implied FE will cause the estimated variance to change, often by a substantial amount and in a downward direction--in which case the corresponding moving-average term may no longer be dominant. There is, however, an alternate and completely objective criterion which yields results that are invariant with respect to such cancellations. By this alternate criterion, the dominant moving-average terms are those containing white noise processes with the largest variances, without regard for the degree of the polynomial in L that multiplies each process and without regard for the sign and size of the coefficients on the various powers of L. Since the estimated variances of the a_t's and the u_t's are as shown in the following table,

Disturbance	Estimated Variance	Estimated Variance Expressed as an Index with Var a_{Gt} = 100
a_{Mt}	.00244	4.3
a_{Gt}	.0562	100.0
a_{kt}	.0000980	0.2
u_{1t}	.00484	8.6
u_{2t}	.00210	3.7
u_{3t}	.00000669	0.1

it is clear that, if this alternate criterion is correct, then moving-average terms containing a_{Gt} will dominate the moving-average parts of the implied FE's. If, in addition, the model is correct, then the moving-average parts of the FE's estimated directly from the data will closely resemble the moving-average terms containing a_{Gt}. Therefore, the adequacy of the model and the appropriateness of this dominance criterion can be tested simultaneously by comparing the modified versions of the implied FE's with the FE's estimated directly from the data. Any significant dissimilarities between the two would indicate that either the model or the dominance criterion, or both, are incorrect.

By this reasoning, the implied FE for log y can be written as

$$(6\text{-}35) \quad (1 - .38L)(1 - .57L)(.75 - .06L) \Delta \log y_t =$$
$$- (1 - .38L)(1 - .57L)(-.069 + .064L)(1 + .45L)a_{Gt},$$

in which all terms other than the one containing a_{Gt} have been omitted, without altering the implied stochastic structure of the process in any significant way. On cancelling the common factors consisting of $(1 - .38L)$ and $(1 - .57L)$, (6-35) becomes:

$$(6\text{-}36) \quad (.75 - .06L) \Delta \log y_t = -(-.069 + .064L)(1 + .45L)a_{Gt}$$
$$= (.069 - .033L - .029L^2)a_{Gt}.$$

Then, dividing through by .75, (6-36) can be expressed as

$$(6\text{-}37) \quad (1 - .08L) \Delta \log y_t = (.092 - .044L - .039L^2)a_{Gt}.$$

Anderson (1976) has shown that a time series consisting of as many as 100 observations may well fail to contain information sufficient to permit identification of ARIMA parameters having values below .2. It is, therefore, very unlikely that ARIMA modeling techniques would detect those parameters in (6-37) having values as low or lower than .08 --especially considering that the length of the relevant time series is only 80 observations. And since these parameters probably will not appear in the estimated FE, they should be eliminated from (6-37) as well.[7] Consequently, the implied FE for log y can be closely approximated by

$$(6\text{-}38) \quad \Delta \log y_t = .092 \, a_{Gt}.$$

---

[7] The coefficient on a_{Gt}, however, cannot be eliminated (by setting it equal to zero) because a_{Gt}, in contrast to a_{Gt-1} and a_{Gt-2}, must appear in the FE.

This suggests that, over the sample period, log y was generated by a random walk process. That this is, in fact, the case was demonstrated earlier. It follows that this particular implication of the model is fully consistent with information contained in the data.

By similar reasoning, the implied FE for log P can be simplified to read

(6-39) $(1 - .38L)(1 - .57L)(.75 - .06L) \Delta \log P_t =$
         $(1 - .38L)(1 - .57L)(.092)(1 + .45L)a_{Gt}$

without altering the process in any fundamental way. On cancelling common factors, (6-39) becomes

(6-40) $(.75 - .06L) \Delta \log P_t = (.092)(1 + .45L)a_{Gt} = (.092 + .041L)a_{Gt}$

or, dividing through by .75,

(6-41) $(1 - .08L) \Delta \log P_t = (.12 + .055L)a_{Gt}.$

Once again, certain of the parameters are so small that it is doubtful they would show up in an ARIMA model fitted directly to the data. Therefore, (6-41) can, for all practical purposes, be written as

(6-42) $\Delta \log P_t = .12 \, a_{Gt},$

which suggests that log P, like log y, was generated by a random walk process. However, the first difference of log P is a realization of a first-order autoregressive process--not white noise, so this implication of the model appears not to be supported by the data.

There is, however, an equally plausible interpretation of the implied FE for log P that is consistent with the data. Suppose that in the transition from (6-39) to (6-40) only the common factor $(1 - .57L)$ had been cancelled, leaving $(1 - .38L)$ on each side. In this event,

(6-39) would have become

(6-43) $(1 - .38L)(.75 - .06L) \Delta \log P_t = (1 - .38L)(.092)(1 + .45L)a_{Gt}$.

Multiplying out both sides of (6-43) and dividing through by .75 yields

(6-44) $(1 - .46L + .030L^2) \Delta \log P_t = (.12 - .10L - .021L^2)a_{Gt}$.

For the reason stated above, (6-44) can be closely approximated by

(6-45) $(1 - .46L) \Delta \log P_t = .12a_{Gt}$,

which is a first-order autoregressive process in $\Delta \log P$. It appears, then, that the implied FE is consistent with both a random walk process in $\log P$ and a first-order autoregressive process in $\Delta \log P$. And since $\Delta \log P$ has, in fact, been generated by a first-order autoregressive process, the implication of the model regarding this variable too is supported by the data. Furthermore, the closeness of the implied and actual autoregressive parameters is nothing short of spectacular. In equation (6-45) the autoregressive parameter is .46, while in the ARIMA model fitted directly to $\log P$ it is .43.

Finally, the implied FE for R can be closely approximated by

(6-46) $(1 - .38L)(1 - .57L)(.75 - .06L) \Delta R_t =$
$(1 - .38L)(1 - .57L)(.0018)(1 + .45L)a_{Gt}$.

On cancelling common factors, (6-46) becomes

(6-47) $(.75 - .06L) \Delta R_t = (.0018)(1 + .45L)a_{Gt} = (.0018 + .00081L)a_{Gt}$

or, dividing through .75,

(6-48) $(1 - .08L) \Delta R_t = (.0024 + .0011L)a_{Gt}$.

Then, discarding variables having near-zero coefficients, (6-48) becomes

(6-49) $\Delta R_t = .0024 a_{Gt}$.

Equation (6-49) implies that, over the sample period, R was generated by a random walk process. This implication, as well, is supported by the data.

As an independent check on the validity of this analysis, a test designed to discriminate among nested ARIMA models was applied to estimates of the implied FE's in an effort to determine whether the simpler versions of these FE's are as consistent with the data as the more complex versions. An affirmative finding would support the contention developed above that the simpler FE's are sufficiently close approximations of the stochastic structure of the endogenous variables. This test, developed by Zellner and Palm (1974), can be described as follows. Let

(6-50) $\hat{\phi}_a(L) Z_t = \hat{\theta}_a(L) \hat{a}_{at}$

be an ARIMA (p_a, d, q_a) model fitted to Z_t, and let $\hat{\sigma}_a^2$ be the corresponding maximum likelihood estimate of the variance of a_{at}. In addition, let

(6-51) $\hat{\phi}_o(L) Z_t = \hat{\theta}_o(L) \hat{a}_{ot}$

be an ARIMA (p_o, d, q_o) model fitted to Z_t, and let $\hat{\sigma}_o^2$ be the maximum likelihood estimate of the variance of a_{ot}. The ratio of the maximized likelihood functions for (6-50) and (6-51), denoted λ, can be expressed as

(6-52) $\lambda = (\hat{\sigma}_o^2 / \hat{\sigma}_a^2)^{T/2}$,

T being the sample size. If it is assumed that $p_o \leq p_a$ and $q_o \leq q_a$ with at least one strict inequality[8] and that (6-51) is the correct

---

[8] If this condition holds, then (6-51) is said to be "nested" in (6-50).

model, then $2 \ln(\lambda)$ is approximately distributed χ^2 with r degrees of freedom--r being the number of restrictions imposed on (6-50) to obtain (6-51). That is, $r = (p_a + q_a) - (p_o + q_o)$. Should $2 \ln(\lambda)$ exceed the critical value for a $\chi^2(r)$ statistic at the chosen level of significance, then the simpler, or nested, model must be rejected in favor of the more complex model. But if $2 \ln(\lambda)$ does not exceed this critical value, it may be concluded that the additional parameters in (6-50) do not significantly improve the fit or that the two models are equally consistent with the data--in which case, by the law of parsimony, the simpler model would be preferred.

To apply this test in the present context, it was first necessary to fit ARIMA models to the more complex versions of the implied FE's. As will be recalled, these more complex versions, given by equations (6-27), (6-29), and (6-31), suggest that both log P and R have been generated by ARIMA (3,1,3) processes and that log y has been generated by an ARIMA (3,1,4) process. Fitted models consistent with these implications appear in Table 6-3. Estimates of the simpler versions of the implied FE's, or equations (6-38), (6-45), and (6-49), were obtained earlier and presented in Table 6-2. Applying the likelihood ratio test described above to these FE's gives the results summarized in Table 6-4.

It is immediately apparent that the simpler models for log P and R fit the data as well as the more complex models--a finding that supports the extension of the Zellner-Palm procedure developed earlier. Only with regard to log y do the results fail to confirm the hypothesis that the simpler model is adequate. However, $2 \ln(\lambda)$ in this case is just barely significant at the 1% level, so the rejection is not that

TABLE 6-3

ESTIMATES OF THE COMPLEX VERSIONS OF THE IMPLIED FINAL EQUATIONS,
UNITED STATES, 1890 TO 1969, ANNUAL DATA

Variable: Logarithm of Real Gross National Product (Log y)
Time Series Process: ARIMA (3,1,4)
Fitted Model:

$$(1-.46L+.61L^2+.32L^3) \Delta \log y_t = .058 + (1-.34L+.76L^2+.45L^3-.079L^4)\hat{a}_{yt}$$
$$(4.43)(10.51)(3.39) \qquad\qquad (6.62) \quad (4.68)(23.80)(7.91)(.66)$$

$R^2 = .26$
D.F. = 71
$\hat{\sigma}^2 = .00322$

Box-Pierce Statistics	Degrees of Freedom	Critical Q Values (10% level of sig.)
Q(12) = 8.6	5	9.2
Q(24) = 15.4	17	24.8

Variable: Logarithm of the Implicit GNP Deflator (Log P)
Time Series Process: ARIMA (3,1,3)
Fitted Model:

$$(1+.22L+.68L^2+.080L^3) \Delta \log P_t = .043 + (1+.66L+1.03L^2+.54L^3)\hat{a}_{Pt}$$
$$(.93)(6.91)(.43) \qquad\qquad (2.26) \quad (3.25)(32.20)(3.03)$$

$R^2 = .26$
D.F. = 72
$\hat{\sigma}^2 = .00220$

Box-Pierce Statistics	Degrees of Freedom	Critical Q Values (10% level of sig.)
Q(12) = 2.4	6	10.6
Q(24) = 14.3	18	26.0

Variable: Long-Term Interest Rate (R)
Time Series Process: ARIMA (3,1,3)
Fitted Model:

$$(1-.89L+.74L^2+.94L^3) \Delta R_t = .00014 + (1+1.01L-.51L^2-.77L^3)\hat{a}_{Rt}$$
$$(35.00)(27.97)(73.31) \qquad\qquad (.75) \quad (17.57)(4.18)(12.79)$$

$R^2 = .14$
D.F. = 72
$\hat{\sigma}^2 = .00000651$

Box-Pierce Statistics	Degrees of Freedom	Critical Q Values (10% level of sig.)
Q(12) = 12.7	6	10.6
Q(24) = 16.4	18	26.0

Note: 1. t-statistics are in parentheses.
2. L is a lag operator such that $L^n x_t = x_{t-n}$.
3. Q(K) is distributed χ^2 with K - p - q degrees of freedom, where p + q equals the number of autoregressive and moving average parameters estimated.

Sources: See Data Appendix.

TABLE 6-4

RESULTS OF LARGE-SAMPLE LIKELIHOOD RATIO TESTS
APPLIED TO FINAL EQUATIONS,
UNITED STATES, 1890 TO 1969, ANNUAL DATA

Models Compared	$\lambda = \left[\dfrac{\hat{\sigma}_0^2}{\hat{\sigma}_a^2}\right]^{T/2}$	$2\ln(\lambda)$	r	$\chi^2_{.05}(r)$
1. Logarithm of Real GNP (Log y) $H_0:(0,1,0)$ vs. $H_a:(3,1,4)$	10,439	18.50	7	14.07
2. Logarithm of the Implicit GNP Deflator (Log P) $H_0:(0,1,0)$ vs. $H_a:(1,1,0)$	1,894	15.09	1	3.84
$H_0:(1,1,0)$ vs. $H_a:(3,1,3)$	4.099	2.82	5	11.07
3. Long-Term Interest Rate (R) $H_0:(0,1,0)$ vs. $H_a:(3,1,3)$	19.67	5.96	6	12.59

Note: 1. $\hat{\sigma}_0^2$ and $\hat{\sigma}_a^2$ are the maximum likelihood estimates of the variances of the white noise processes in the ARIMA representations designated H_0 and H_a, respectively.

2. T(=79) is the number of observations used to estimate the ARIMA models.

3. r is the number of restrictions imposed on H_a to obtain H_0. Thus, $r = (p_a + q_a) - (p_0 + q_0)$.

4. $\chi^2_{.05}(r)$ is the critical value of a χ^2 statistic with r degrees of freedom at the 5% level of significance.

5. $2\ln(\lambda)$ is approximately distributed $\chi^2(r)$.

striking. On balance, these results do appear to support the simpler versions of the implied FE's described above. In addition, a likelihood ratio test applied to ARIMA (1,1,0) and (0,1,0) models for log P indicates that the random walk model is inadequate. This is the same conclusion reached earlier using the Box-Jenkins techniques, and it supports the contention that the proper form of the implied FE for log P is given by equation (6-45) and not by equation (6-42).

In summary, the implications of the model regarding the time series properties of the endogenous variables are in substantial, if not complete, agreement with information contained in the data, and confidence in the adequacy of the model is greatly increased. In the following chapter, the model is shown to imply a Gibson Paradox-type relationship between the interest rate and the price level, and the source of this relationship is identified.

CHAPTER VII

THE GIBSON PARADOX RE-EXAMINED

Using an extension of the procedure developed by Zellner and Palm, implications of the model developed in Chapter 5 regarding the time series properties of real income, the price level, and the interest rate have been examined and found consistent with the data. Naturally, this finding increases the confidence with which other implications of the model are viewed. As it turns out, the model also implies the existence of a Gibson Paradox-type relationship between the interest rate and the price level. Moreover, this relationship is found to extend to the level of real income, suggesting that the Gibson Paradox is not an isolated phenomenon, but an element of a larger set of relationships among economic variables.

These implications stand out dramatically in the simpler versions of the implied FE's for log y, log P, and R which, for convenience, are reproduced below:

(7-1) $\Delta \log y_t = .092 a_{Gt}$

(7-2) $(1 - .46L) \Delta \log P_t = .12 a_{Gt}$

(7-3) $\Delta R_t = .0024 a_{Gt}$

It is immediately apparent that these FE's suggest a solution to the Gibson Paradox since a "pip" in a_{Gt} will cause $\log y_t$, $\log P_t$, and R_t to move in the same direction. Moreover, this explanation of the phenomenon has a straightforward and appealing interpretation in terms of the familiar IS-LM, aggregate demand-aggregate supply framework. To see this, it should be recalled that a_{Gt} is the innovation in the stochastic process generating (the logarithm of) nominal government purchases of goods and services. That is, a_{Gt} is the part of log G_t that cannot be predicted from its own history. An unexpected increase in log G_t (which corresponds to $a_{Gt} > 0$) shifts the IS and aggregate demand schedules to the right, causing real income, the price level, and the interest rate to rise. An unexpected decrease in log G_t yields the opposite result. Thus, variations in a_{Gt} are certainly capable of producing the observed correlation between the interest rate and the price level. Furthermore, this explanation of the phenomenon is entirely consistent with orthodox economic theory.

It would be desirable, as a final check on the validity of this analysis, to compare the correlations between $\Delta \log y_t$, $\Delta \log P_t$, and ΔR_t that are implied by equations (7-1), (7-2), and (7-3) with the actual correlations between the same variables. If the FE's do, in fact, capture the essence of the Gibson Paradox, then the implied correlations should be close to the actual correlations. It is clear from an examination of the FE's, however, that each of the implied correlations is precisely equal to one. The actual correlations, on the other hand, are much lower, as shown by Table 7-1 below.

It would be a mistake to conclude, however, that the simplified FE's are inadequate. The reason is that the implied correlations are those that would result if a_{Gt} were the only disturbance acting on the system. But, of course, a_{Gt} is not the only disturbance. It is embedded in a whole series of white noise processes acting on the

TABLE 7-1

CORRELATIONS BETWEEN $\Delta \log y_t$, $\Delta \log P_t$, AND ΔR_t,
UNITED STATES, 1890 TO 1969, ANNUAL DATA

	$\Delta \log y$	$\Delta \log P$	ΔR
$\Delta \log y$	1.00		
$\Delta \log P$	.30	1.00	
ΔR	-.15	.20	1.00

endogenous variables.[1] The effect of these other disturbances is to cause the variances of $\Delta \log y_t$, $\Delta \log P_t$, and ΔR_t to be higher than those implied by the simplified FE's, without necessarily causing the covariances between the same variables to be higher as well. As a result, eliminating the non-dominant disturbances from the FE's reduces the implied variances, but not necessarily the implied covariances, and therefore causes the simplified FE's to overstate the true correlations.[2] It follows that a better procedure for checking the accuracy of the implied statistical relationships between the endogenous variables is to compare the covariances implied by equations (7-1), (7-2), and (7-3) with the actual covariances.[3]

---

[1] See the complex versions of the implied FE's on page 78.

[2] Since Correlation $(X,Y) = \dfrac{\text{Covariance } (X,Y)}{\sqrt{\sigma_X^2 \cdot \sigma_Y^2}}$, a reduction in in σ_X^2 and/or σ_Y^2 without a commensurate reduction in Covar(X,Y) necessarily increases Corr(X,Y).

[3] To see this point more clearly, suppose that the final equations for the time series variables Δx_t and Δy_t are

$$\Delta x_t = a_t + b_t \quad \text{and}$$

$$\Delta y_t = a_t + c_t,$$

In order to make this comparison, it is necessary to calculate the implied covariances. Thus[4]

---

where a_t, b_t, and c_t are independent white noise processes. The covariance and the correlation between Δx_t and Δy_t are

$$\text{Covar}(\Delta x_t, \Delta y_t) = \text{Var } a_t \quad \text{and}$$

$$\text{Corr}(\Delta x_t, \Delta y_t) = \frac{\text{Var } a_t}{\sqrt{(\text{Var } a_t + \text{Var } b_t)(\text{Var } a_t + \text{Var } c_t)}}.$$

If a_t is the dominant white noise process in each FE, then the following simplified versions of the FE's adequately represent the statistical structure of each variable:

$$\Delta x_t = a_t \quad \text{and}$$

$$\Delta y_t = a_t.$$

The covariance and the correlation implied by these simplified FE's are

$$\text{Covar}(\Delta x_t, \Delta y_t) = \text{Var } a_t \quad \text{and}$$

$$\text{Corr}(\Delta x_t, \Delta y_t) = 1.$$

Notice that the implied covariance is invariant with respect to elimination of the non-dominant white noise process in each FE. The implied correlation, however, is not invariant. Thus, the simplified versions of the FE's accurately capture the covariance between Δx_t and Δy_t but not the correlation between the same variables. While this example is not precisely equivalent to the problem discussed in the text (in particular, the non-dominant white noise processes in the implied FE's for $\Delta \log y_t$, $\Delta \log P_t$, and ΔR_t are not independent within or across equations), it is a fairly close approximation. Consequently, it supports the argument that the statistical adequacy of the simplified versions of the implied FE's can be better assessed by comparing the implied and actual covariances between $\Delta \log y_t$, $\Delta \log P_t$, and ΔR_t than by comparing the implied and actual correlations. The reason is that the simplified FE's are more likely to contain good estimates of the true covariances than they are to contain good estimates of the true correlations.

[4] In all of the following calculations, $\text{Var}(\hat{a}_{Gt})$ is substituted for $\text{Var}(a_{Gt})$, which is unknown.

(7-4) $\text{Covar}(\Delta \log y_t, \Delta \log P_t) = E[(.092\, a_{Gt})(\frac{.12}{1-.46L}\, a_{Gt})]$

$$= \frac{.011}{1-.46L} E(a_{Gt}^2) = \frac{.011}{1-.46L} \text{Var}(a_{Gt})$$

$$= \frac{.00062}{1-.46L}.$$

Multiplying through by $(1-.46L)$, (7-4) becomes

(7-5) $(1-.46L) \text{Covar}(\Delta \log y_t, \Delta \log P_t) = .00062.$

But since $\text{Covar}(\Delta \log y_t, \Delta \log P_t) = \text{Covar}(\Delta \log y_{t-1}, \Delta \log P_{t-1})$, (7-5) can be written equivalently as

(7-6) $(1-.46) \text{Covar}(\Delta \log y_t, \Delta \log P_t) = .00062,$

so that

(7-7) $\text{Covar}(\Delta \log y_t, \Delta \log P_t) = \frac{.00062}{.54} = .0011.$

By precisely the same reasoning, it can be shown that

(7-8) $\text{Covar}(\Delta \log P_t, \Delta R_t) = .000030.$

Finally,

(7-9) $\text{Covar}(\Delta \log y_t, \Delta R_t) = E[(.092\, a_{Gt})(.0024\, a_{Gt})] = .00022\, E(a_{Gt}^2)$

$$= .00022\, \text{Var}(a_{Gt}) = .000012.$$

These results are collected in Table 7-2 below, which also shows the actual covariances.

The implied covariances between $\Delta \log y_t$ and $\Delta \log P_t$ and between $\Delta \log P_t$ and ΔR_t are very close to the actual values, indicating that the model does, in fact, capture the essence of the statistical relationships between these variables. Only in the case of $\Delta \log y_t$ and ΔR_t do the FE's fail to mimic the true relationship. While this is a disturbing result, it should be noted that the implied covariance is only slightly in excess of zero. So it is not wholly unreasonable to assume that some other disturbance (or disturbances) acting on the system has converted what would otherwise have been a small, positive covariance into a small, negative one. Nonetheless, the accuracy of the implied covariances in the other two cases, one of which represents the Gibson Paradox, is most encouraging, and it indicates that the model does, indeed, explain some significant empirical phenomena.

TABLE 7-2

COVARIANCES BETWEEN Δ LOG y_t, Δ LOG P_t, AND ΔR_t,
ACTUAL AND IMPLIED,
UNITED STATES, 1890 TO 1969, ANNUAL DATA

	Actual	Implied	Percent Difference
Covar(Δ log y_t, Δ log P_t)	.00099	.0011	11.1%
Covar(Δ log P_t, ΔR_t)	.000028	.000030	7.1%
Covar(Δ log y_t, ΔR_t)	-.000025	.000012	n.a.

n.a. = not applicable

To summarize, the simplified versions of the implied FE's indicate that the Gibson Paradox has been produced by fluctuations in aggregate demand deriving from innovations in nominal government purchases of goods and services. Graphically, this explanation can be described as a shifting IS schedule which, as is well known, causes real income, the price level, and the interest rate to move in the same direction. This interpretation of the phenomenon is entirely consistent with orthodox economic theory. Furthermore, it should be noted that, if this explanation is correct, the Gibson Paradox is a real phenomenon, since it has been produced by disturbances originating in the real sector. As such, it is fundamentally a relationship between the price level and the real rate of interest, although, to the extent that movements in the real rate are reflected in the nominal rate, the latter will exhibit the Paradox as well.

CHAPTER VIII

CONCLUSION

The Gibson Paradox is an empirical regularity consisting of the positive correlation between the interest rate and the price level. While this relationship may or may not be paradoxical in the generally accepted sense of the word, a satisfactory explanation of the phenomenon has never been advanced, although there has been no shortage of candidates. It has been the intent of this dissertation to provide a fresh approach to the study of the Paradox and, in so doing, to provide at least the outlines of a solution, if not a complete explanation.

This dissertation began with an examination of long-term interest rate and wholesale price data for nine countries. Correlations between these two series, reported in Table 2-1, demonstrate that the Gibson Paradox does indeed exist and, furthermore, that it is a widespread phenomenon. Additional evidence presented in Table 2-3 consisting of correlations between detrended interest rate and wholesale price data suggests that long-term trends have little or nothing to do with the Paradox. In fact, linear trends in the two series have frequently been in opposite directions, causing the observed correlation to be weaker, not stronger. A more detailed examination of the data for Great Britain and the United States was conducted by dividing the sample for each country into subperiods corresponding to identifiable swings in long-term bond yields. Correlations between raw and detrended interest rates and wholesale prices were calculated for each subperiod and reported in Tables 2-4 and 2-5. These correlations indicate that the Gibson Paradox is a composite of short- and intermediate-term covariations in interest rates and prices, with the latter accounting for the major share of the overall correlation. It was noted that the correct explanation of the phenomenon ought to be consistent with these findings.

Then, the two most prominent of the many explanations of the Gibson Paradox, one attributed to Irving Fisher and the other jointly to Knut Wicksell and J. M. Keynes, were examined. Each was found not to be supported by the available empirical evidence. A more intensive test of the Fisher explanation was conducted by regressing the rate of interest on an index of wholesale prices and a proxy for the expected rate of change in prices.[1] If this explanation is correct, then the price expectations proxy should be positively related to the rate of interest. Moreover, this association should be stronger than that between the price level and the interest rate since it is changes in expectations that, in the Fisher explanation, are alleged to have produced interest rate movements that happen to conform with movements in the price level. The results of these regressions, presented in Table 4A-1, are inconsistent with the Fisher explanation. Not only is the partial correlation between the proxy for price expectations and the interest rate lower than the partial correlation between the price level and the interest rate, but it is not even generally positive. Once the existing positive relationship between the interest rate and

---

[1] This proxy is ($\log \text{WPI}^e_{t+1} - \log \text{WPI}_t$), where $\log \text{WPI}^e_{t+1}$ is the forecast of $\log \text{WPI}_{t+1}$ derived from the univariate ARIMA model fitted to a wholesale price index for each country.

the price level is taken into account, changes in that level appear to be entirely unrelated to the interest rate or, at least, unrelated in the usual Fisherian sense. An important conclusion deriving from this discussion was that the "Fisher effect" on nominal interest rates is not an important aspect of the correct explanation of the Gibson Paradox and, therefore, that the fundamental relationship is between the price level and the real rate of interest.

The simplest alternate hypothesis that provides a rational theoretical basis for the phenomenon is that there exists a strictly bivariate relationship between the interest rate and the price level such that high (low) prices directly "cause" high (low) interest rates and/or vice versa. If this were the correct explanation of the Paradox, then it would be appropriate to estimate the relationship between these two variables by regressing one on the other. Regressions of this type, with the interest rate as the left-hand variable, were originally reported in Table 2-3 in connection with a description of the data. However, if these equations are to be given behavioral content, then the extremely low Durbin-Watson statistics become a matter of some concern since the usual significance tests on the estimated coefficients are invalid in the presence of autocorrelation. Therefore, each of these equations was re-estimated using the Cochrane-Orcutt iterative technique, and the results were presented in Table 4-1. The autocorrelation-corrected regressions are inconsistent with the strictly bivariate hypothesis because they generally imply lower correlations between the two series than actually exist.

A different explanation of the Gibson Paradox that was suggested by these results is that the phenomenon is an example of "spurious correlation" between two highly-autocorrelated, but independent, time series. However, "spurious correlation" cannot explain the preponderance of positive correlations that exists across countries unless interest rates and prices tend to drift upward or downward together over time. And that this is not the case was suggested earlier by the regressions of detrended interest rates on detrended prices reported in Table 2-3. Nonetheless, this interpretation of the phenomenon was examined more carefully by cross-correlating the residuals from univariate ARIMA models fitted to each series. Since these residuals, which are non-autocorrelated and trend-free by construction, were significantly and positively correlated, the "spurious regression" hypothesis was discredited. In addition, the non-uniform pattern of these cross-correlations across countries further suggested that the strictly bivariate hypothesis is incorrect, if it is true, as seems reasonable, that a strictly bivariate relationship would have produced a uniform pattern. The results of these tests were summarized in Table 4-4.

The immediate implication of these findings was that the observed correlation between the interest rate and the price level must be the result of mutual correlation with a third variable, or perhaps a set of variables. In turn, this suggested a macroeconomic model in which the interest rate and the price level are two of the endogenous variables. It seemed clear that an analysis of the true specification of this model could yield some insights regarding the source of the Gibson Paradox, if not the source itself.

Therefore, a small macroeconomic model incorporating the interest rate and the price level as endogenous variables was derived from an explicit, and quite orthodox, system of structural equations. Three-stage least squares estimates of the model equations using annual United States data were reported in Table 5-1. Then, a relatively new and powerful technique combining time series analysis with traditional econometrics was used to develop the implications of the model regarding the time series properties of the endogenous variables. Initially, the model was found to imply final equations[2] for real income, the price level, and the interest rate corresponding to autoregressive integrated moving average (3,1,4), (3,1,3), and (3,1,3) processes, respectively. However, as Table 6-2 indicates, the stochastic structure of the price level is that of an integrated first-order autoregressive process, while real income and the interest rate appear to be realizations of random walk processes. Thus, it appeared that the implications of the model were inconsistent with information contained in the data. But it was shown that the moving-average parts of the implied final equations are dominated by a single white noise process, so that a reasonable simplification of each equation could be obtained by eliminating the terms containing non-dominant processes. When this was done, the simplified versions of the final equations were found to be consistent with univariate ARIMA models fitted directly to the data, and confidence in the model was greatly enhanced.

What is more important, this analysis revealed the model to imply a Gibson Paradox-type relationship between the interest rate and the price level. This relationship stands out dramatically in the simplified

---

[2] The final equations of a model express the endogenous variables in ARIMA form as functions of the autoregressive and moving-average parts of the processes generating the exogenous variables, the model parameters, the innovations in the processes generating the exogenous variables, and the disturbances in the model equations.

versions of the implied final equations which are reproduced below:

$$\Delta \log y_t = .092\, a_{Gt}$$
$$(1 - .46L)\, \Delta \log P_t = .12\, a_{Gt}$$
and
$$\Delta R_t = .0024\, a_{Gt},$$

where y_t, P_t, and R_t are real income, the price level, and the interest rate, respectively, and a_{Gt} is the innovation in the stochastic process generating nominal government purchases of goods and services. That is, a_{Gt} is the component of government purchases that cannot be predicted from the history of the same series. It is immediately apparent that these final equations suggest a solution to the Gibson Paradox since a "pip" in a_{Gt} will cause $\log y_t$, $\log P_t$, and R_t to move in the same direction. Moreover, this relationship is seen to extend to the level of real income, indicating that the Gibson Paradox is not an isolated phenomenon, but rather is an integral part of a wider set of economic relationships.

This explanation of the Paradox has a straightforward and appealing interpretation in terms of the familiar IS-LM, aggregate demand-aggregate supply framework. A positive innovation in nominal government purchases of goods and services shifts the IS and aggregate demand schedules to the right, causing real income, the price level, and the interest rate to rise. An unexpected decrease yields the opposite result. Thus, innovations in government purchases certainly appear to be capable of generating the observed correlation between the interest rate and the price level. In addition, this explanation does not depend on coincident trends, and there is no reason why it should not be consistent with an overall correlation between the two series that appears to be a composite of short- and intermediate-term correlations. Furthermore, if this explanation is correct, then the Gibson Paradox is fundamentally a relationship between the price level and the real rate of interest, although, to the extent that movements in the real rate are reflected by movements in the nominal rate, the latter will exhibit the Paradox as well. As a final check on the validity of this analysis, the covariance between the United States interest rate and price level that is implied by the simplified versions of the final equations was derived and compared with the actual covariance over the sample period. The difference between the two was found to be less than eight percent.

In retrospect, the solution to the Gibson Paradox seems remarkably simple. Indeed, it was suggested earlier by Tobin (1968) and Sargent (1973b), and it bears striking similarities to the explanation offered by Keynes (1930) and Wicksell (1935). But the empirical validity of this explanation has never been demonstrated in a convincing manner. Perhaps the main reason for the difficulties that economists have encountered in attempting to explain the Paradox is their failure to view the phenomenon in its proper perspective which, as has been shown in this dissertation, is that of an economic system which contains the interest rate and the price level as endogenous variables. Within this broader context, the Paradox is easily seen to be an integral part of a wider set of relationships among economic variables rather than an isolated phenomenon. The correlation between the interest rate and the price level, however, has been the only one of these relationships singled out for special attention, apparently because only it has ever been considered paradoxical. One cannot help but think that the Gibson Paradox would have been solved long ago had this not been the case.

APPENDIX A

Plots of Autocorrelation and Partial Autocorrelation Functions
Estimated from First Differences of
Long-Term Interest Rate and Wholesale Price Data,
Eight Countries, Selected Periods, Annual Data

Note: All autocorrelation and partial autocorrelation functions pertaining to Wholesale Price Indexes were estimated using logarithmic data.

Estimated Autocorrelation Function,
First Difference of Wholesale Price Index,
Belgium, 1832 to 1913, Annual Data

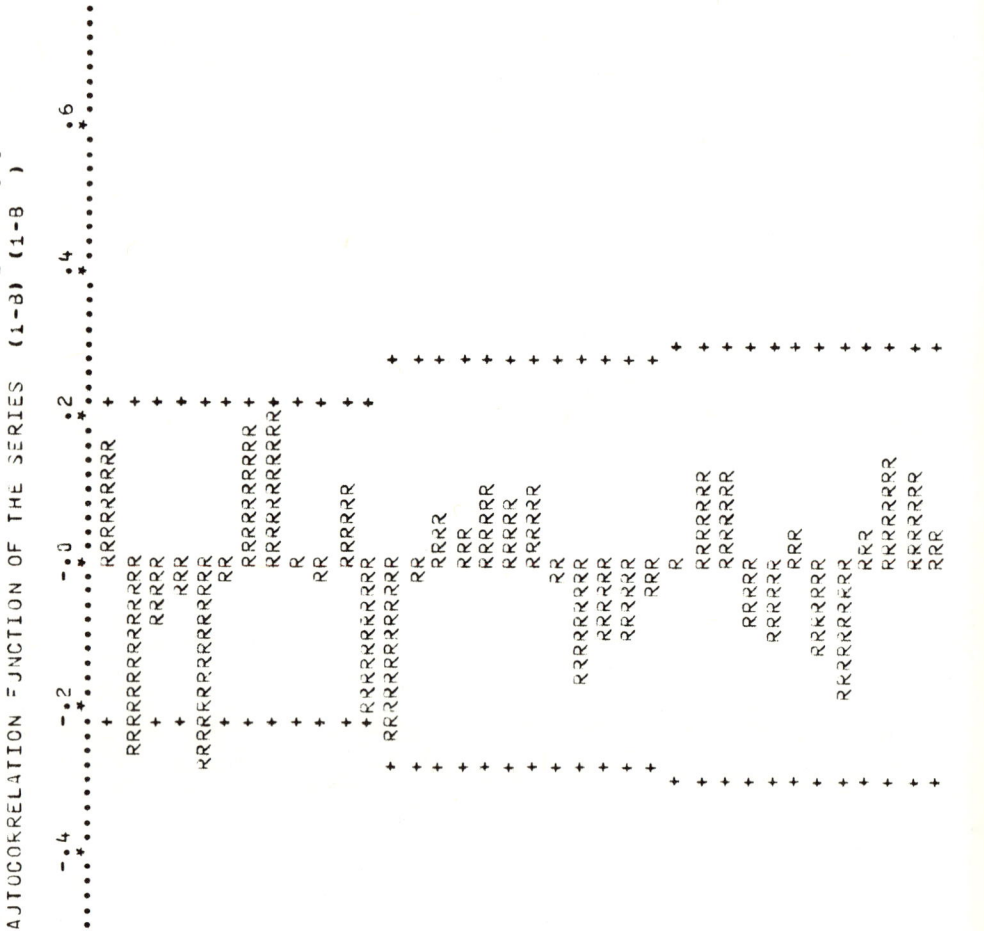

Estimated Partial Autocorrelation Function,
First Difference of Wholesale Price Index,
Belgium, 1832 to 1913, Annual Data

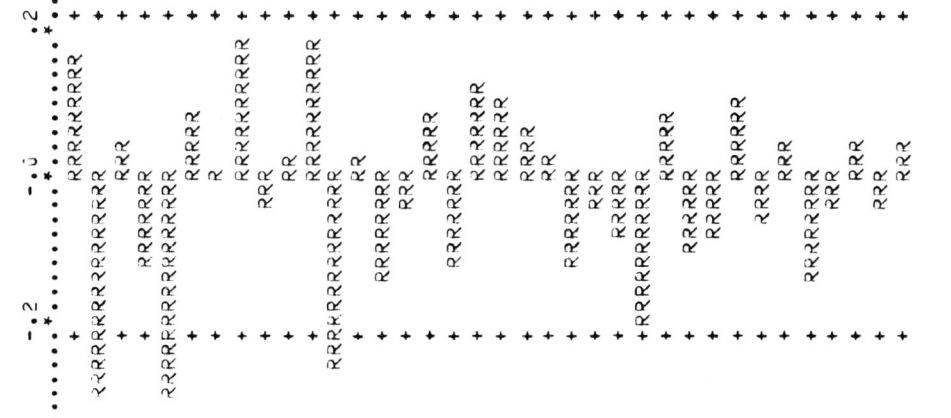

Estimated Autocorrelation Function,
First Difference of Long-Term Interest Rate,
Belgium, 1831 to 1913, Annual Data

Estimated Partial Autocorrelation Function,
First Difference of Long-Term Interest Rate,
Belgium, 1831 to 1913, Annual Data

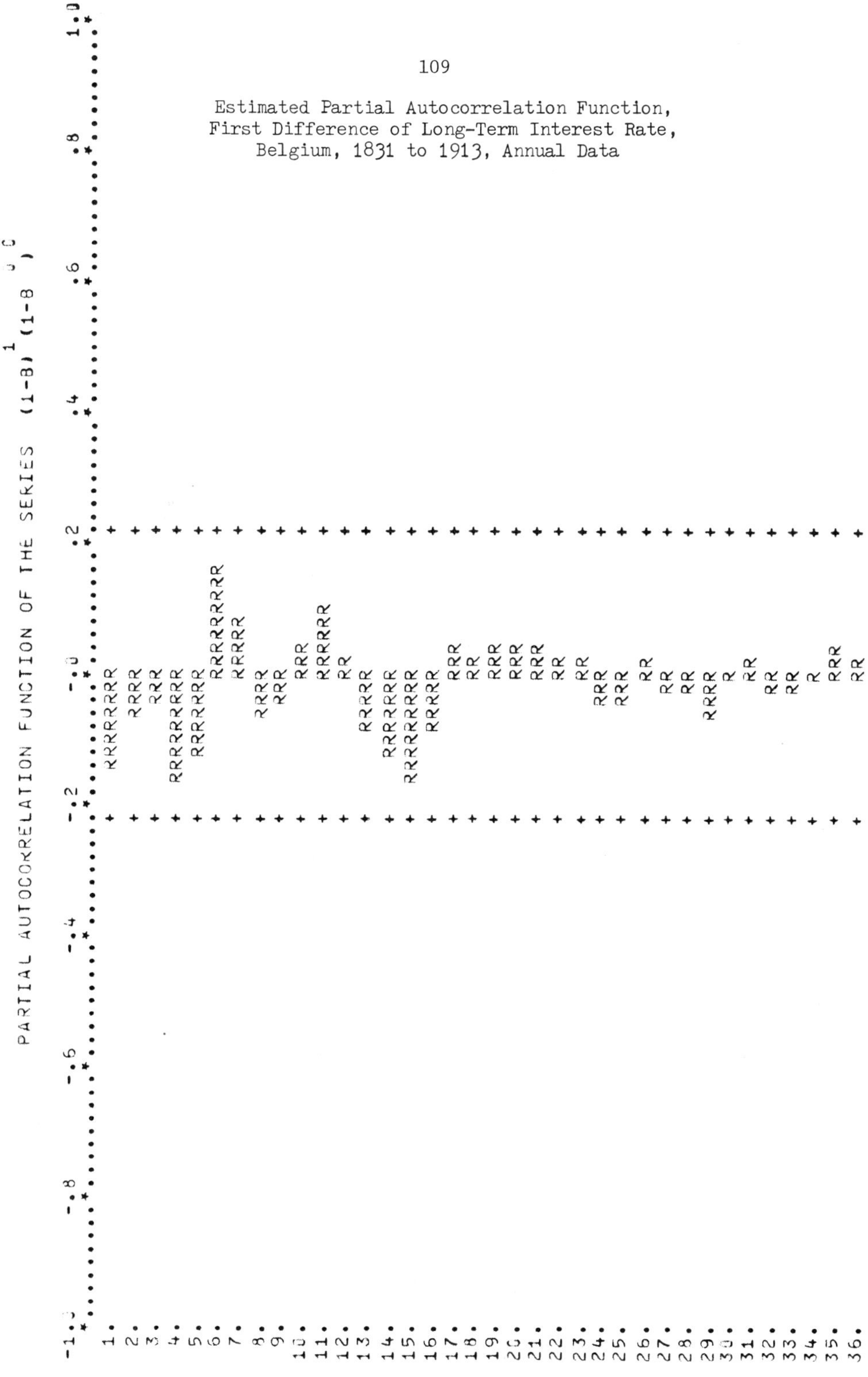

Estimated Autocorrelation Function,
First Difference of Wholesale Price Index,
Canada, 1867 to 1974, Annual Data

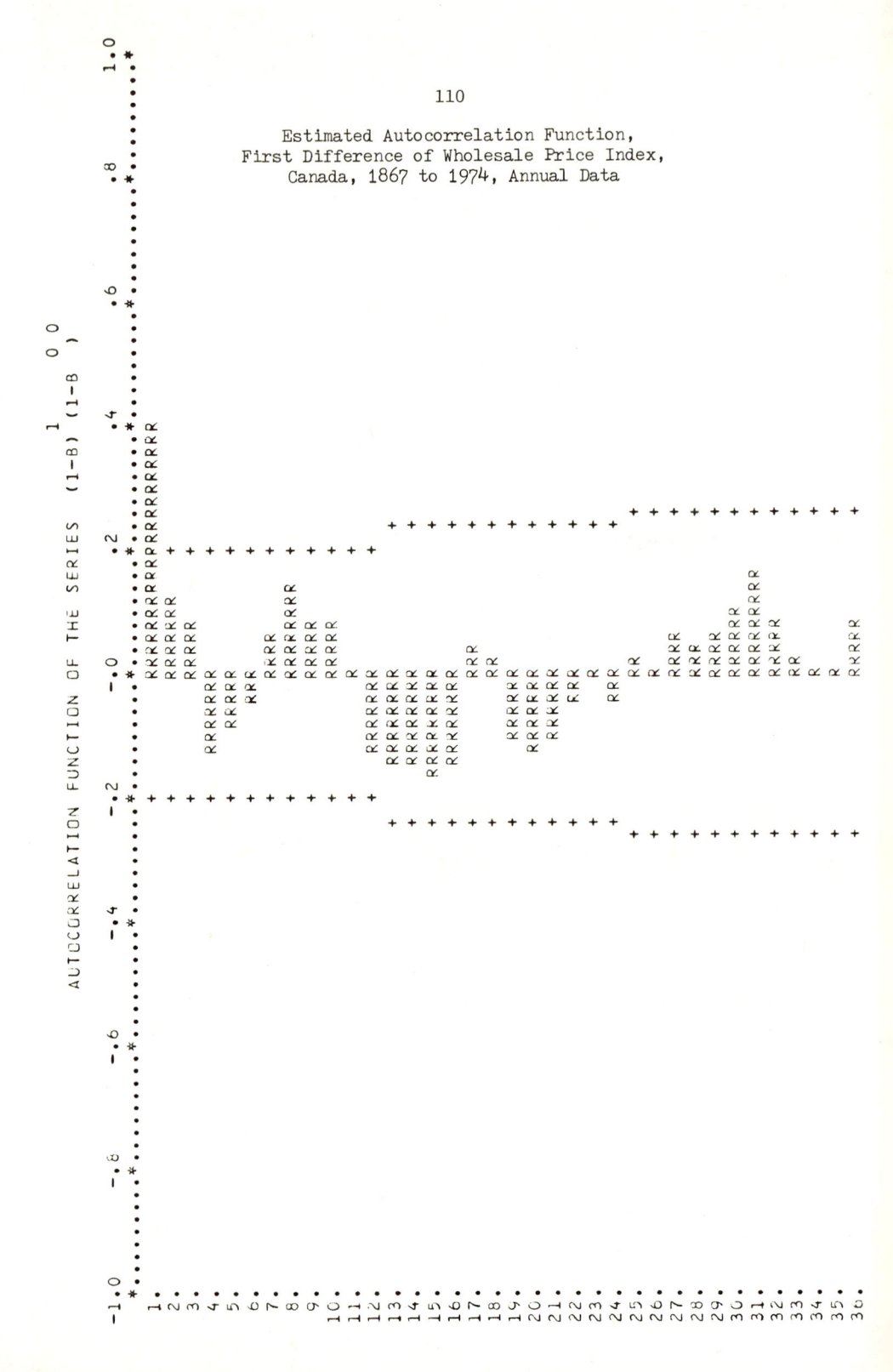

Estimated Partial Autocorrelation Function,
First Difference of Wholesale Price Index,
Canada, 1867 to 1974, Annual Data

Estimated Autocorrelation Function,
First Difference of Long-Term Interest Rate,
Canada, 1900 to 1974, Annual Data

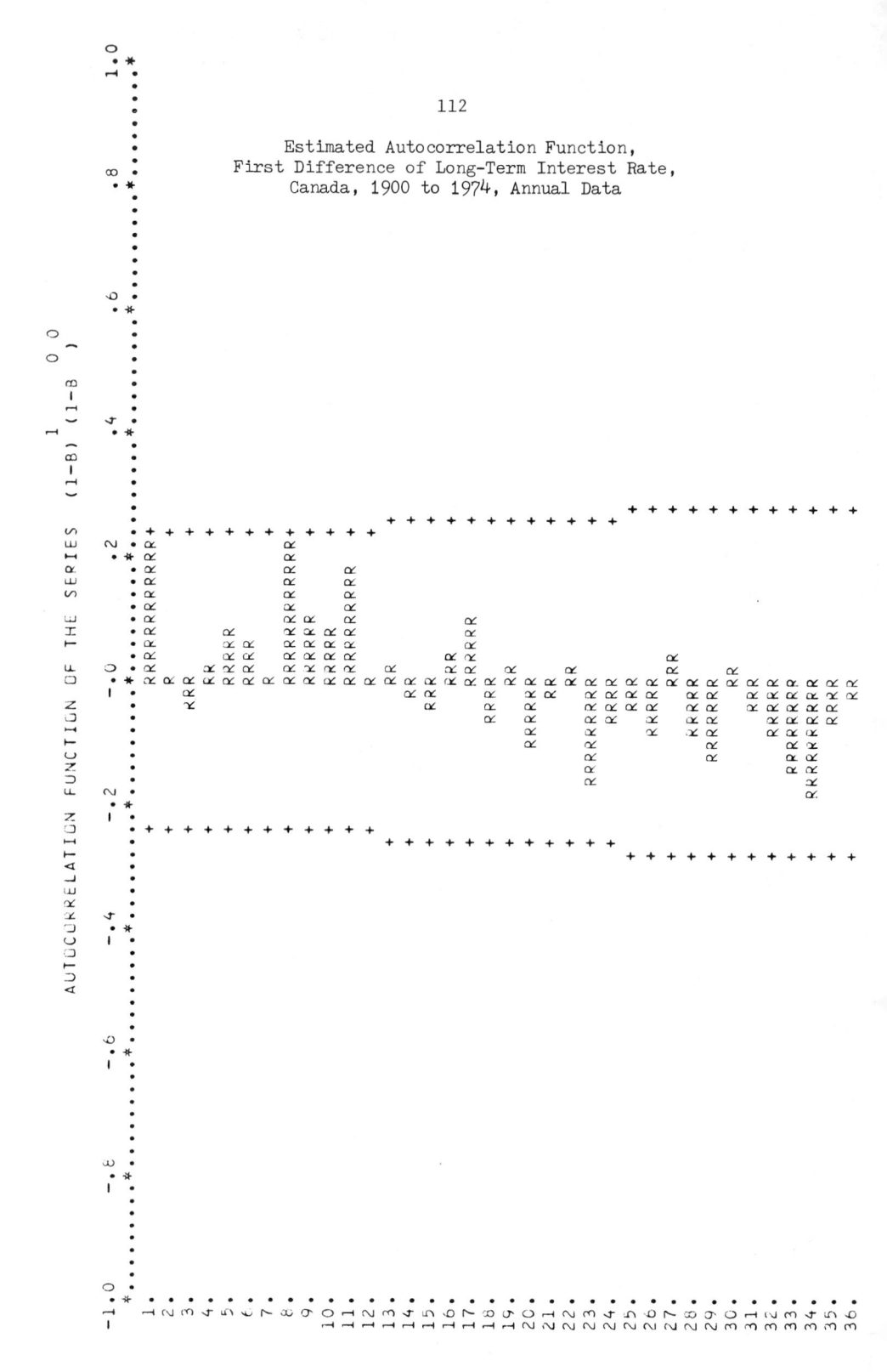

Estimated Partial Autocorrelation Function,
First Difference of Long-Term Interest Rate,
Canada, 1900 to 1974, Annual Data

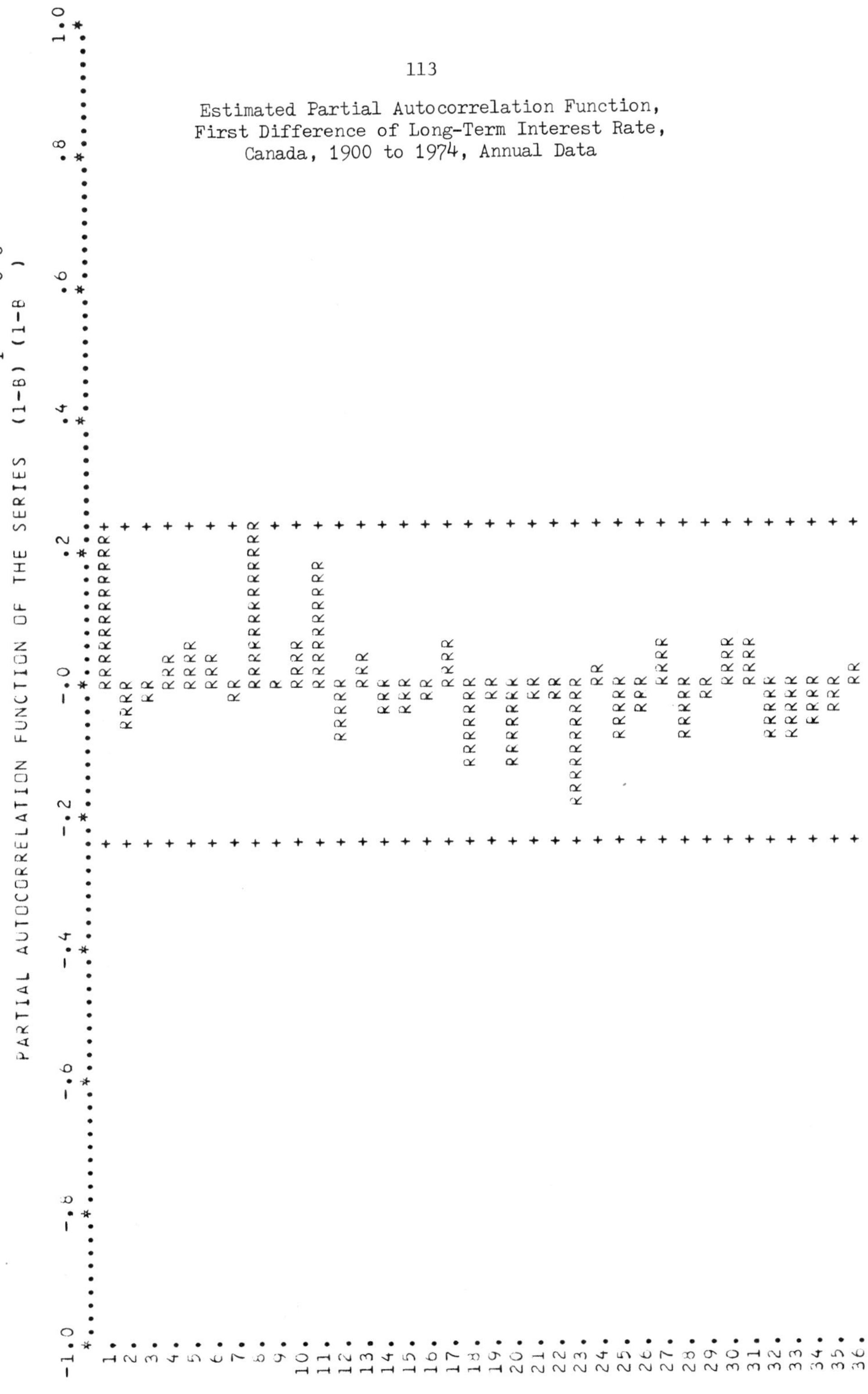

Estimated Autocorrelation Function
First Difference of Wholesale Price Index,
France, 1798 to 1914, Annual Data

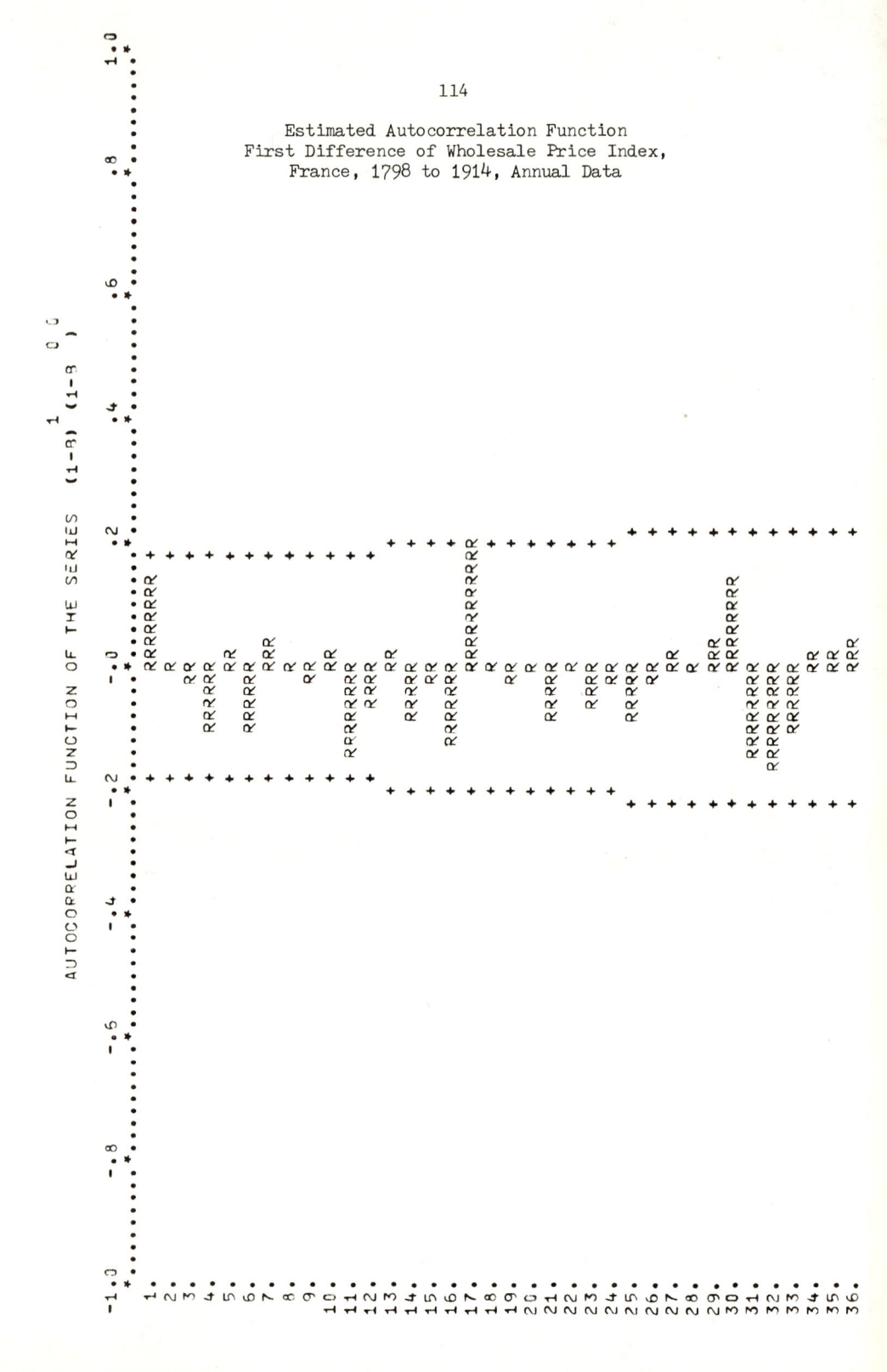

Estimated Partial Autocorrelation Function,
First Difference of Wholesale Price Index,
France, 1798 to 1914, Annual Data

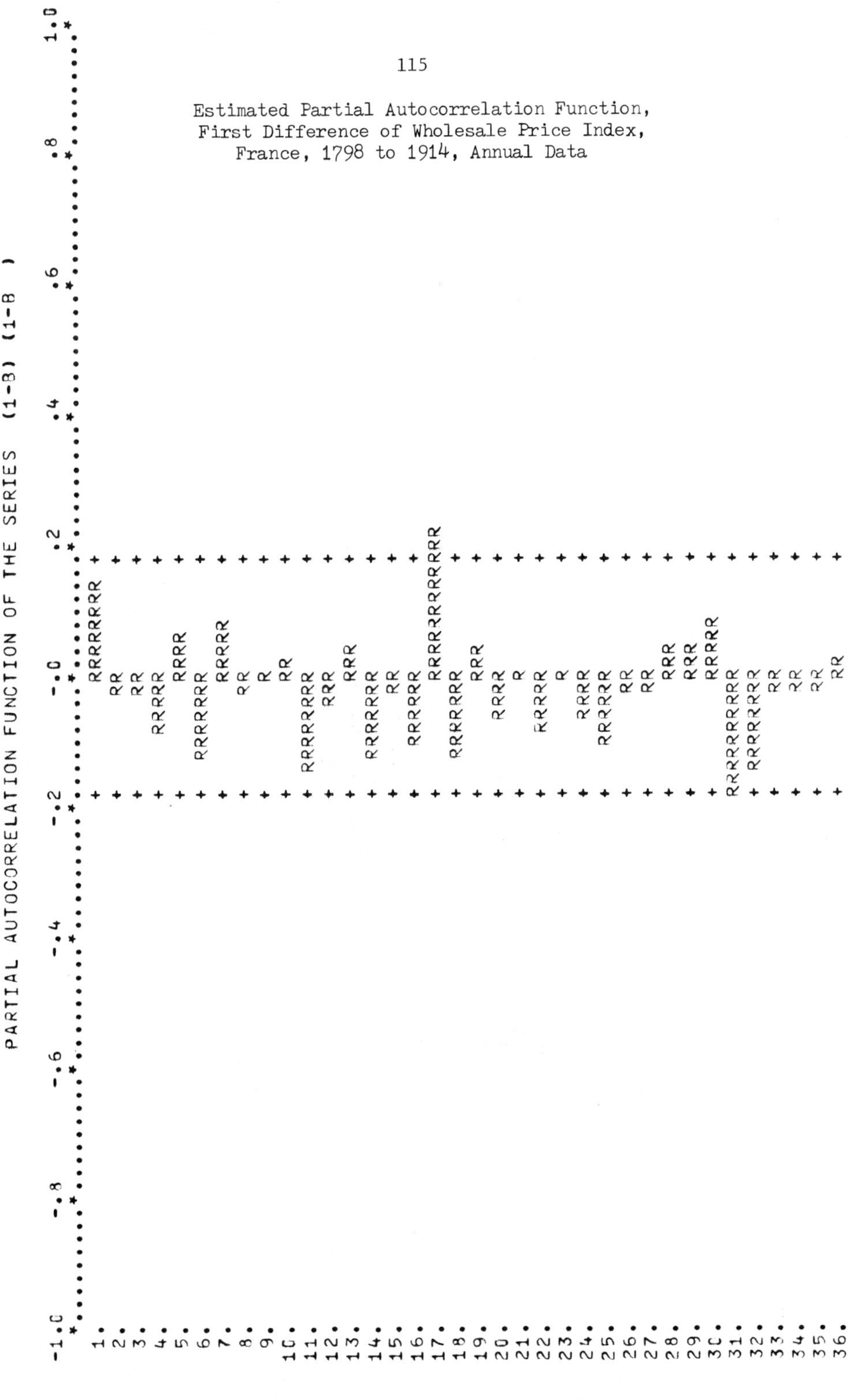

Estimated Autocorrelation Function,
First Difference of Wholesale Price Index,
France, 1914 to 1974, Annual Data

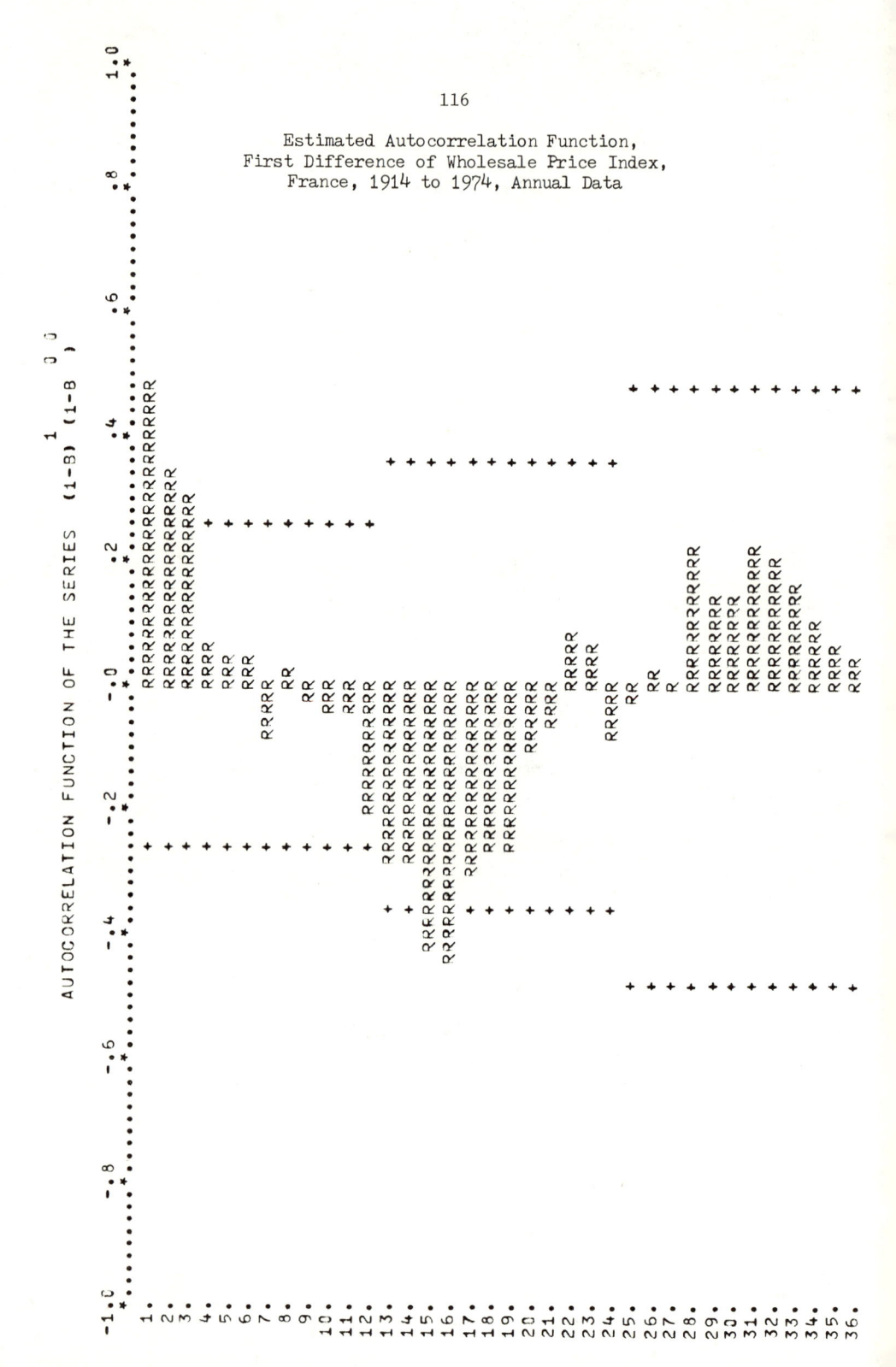

Estimated Partial Autocorrelation Function,
First Difference of Wholesale Price Index,
France, 1914 to 1974, Annual Data

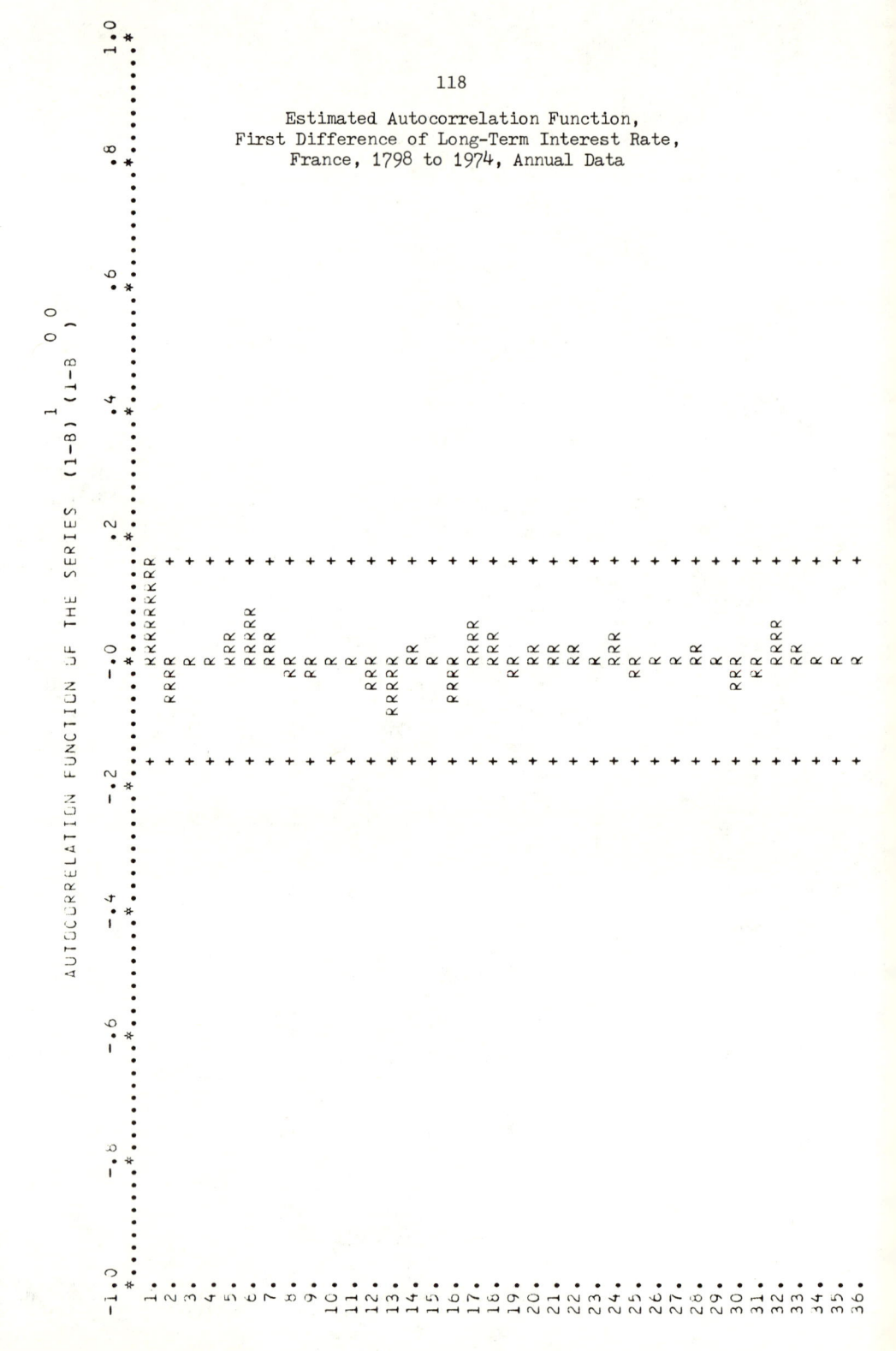

Estimated Autocorrelation Function,
First Difference of Long-Term Interest Rate,
France, 1798 to 1974, Annual Data

Estimated Partial Autocorrelation Function,
First Difference of Long-Term Interest Rate,
France, 1798 to 1974, Annual Data

Estimated Autocorrelation Function,
First Difference of Wholesale Price Index,
Germany, 1792 to 1921, Annual Data

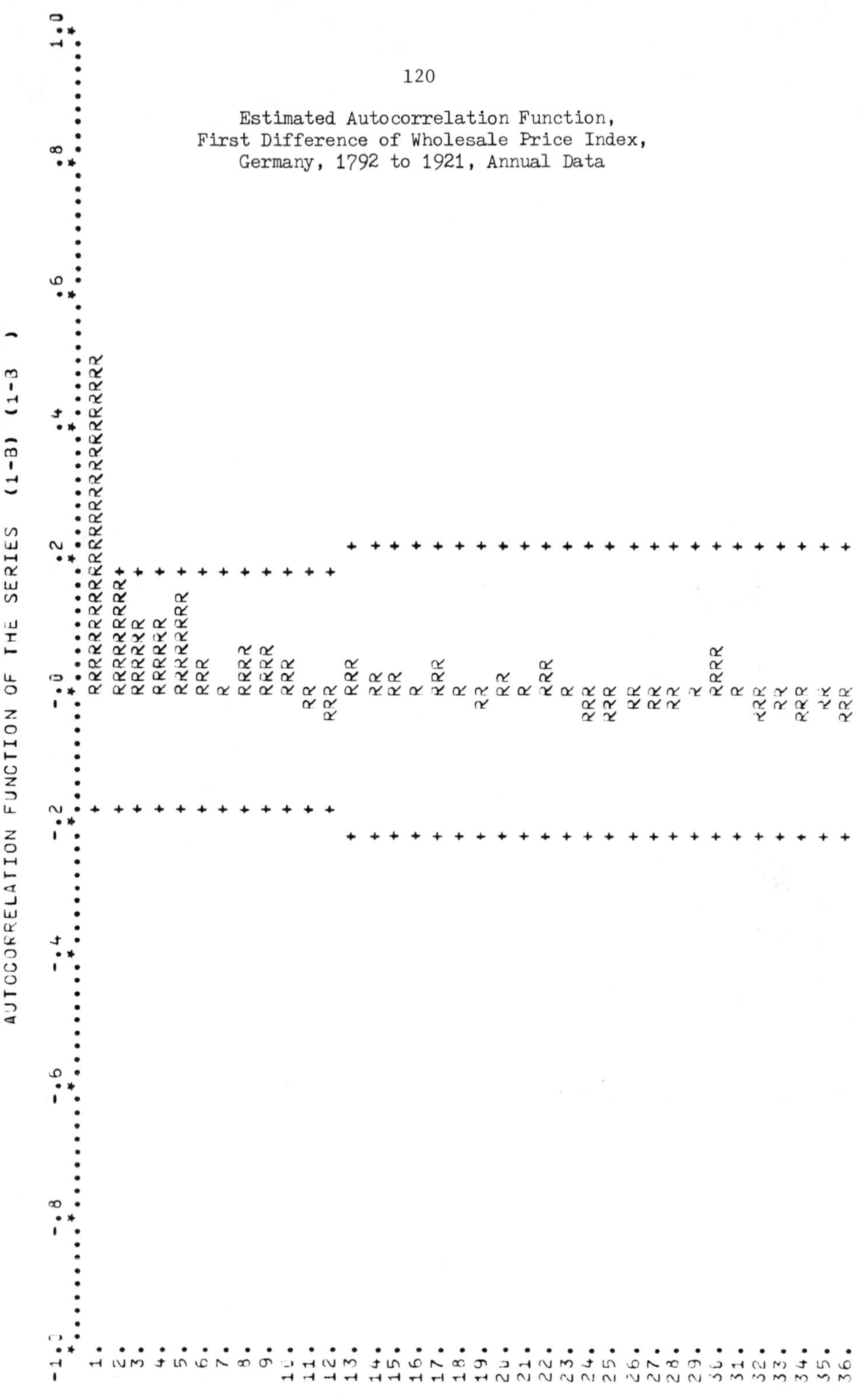

Estimated Partial Autocorrelation Function
First Difference of Wholesale Price Index,
Germany, 1792 to 1921, Annual Data

Estimated Autocorrelation Function,
First Difference of Long-Term Interest Rate,
Germany, 1815 to 1921, Annual Data

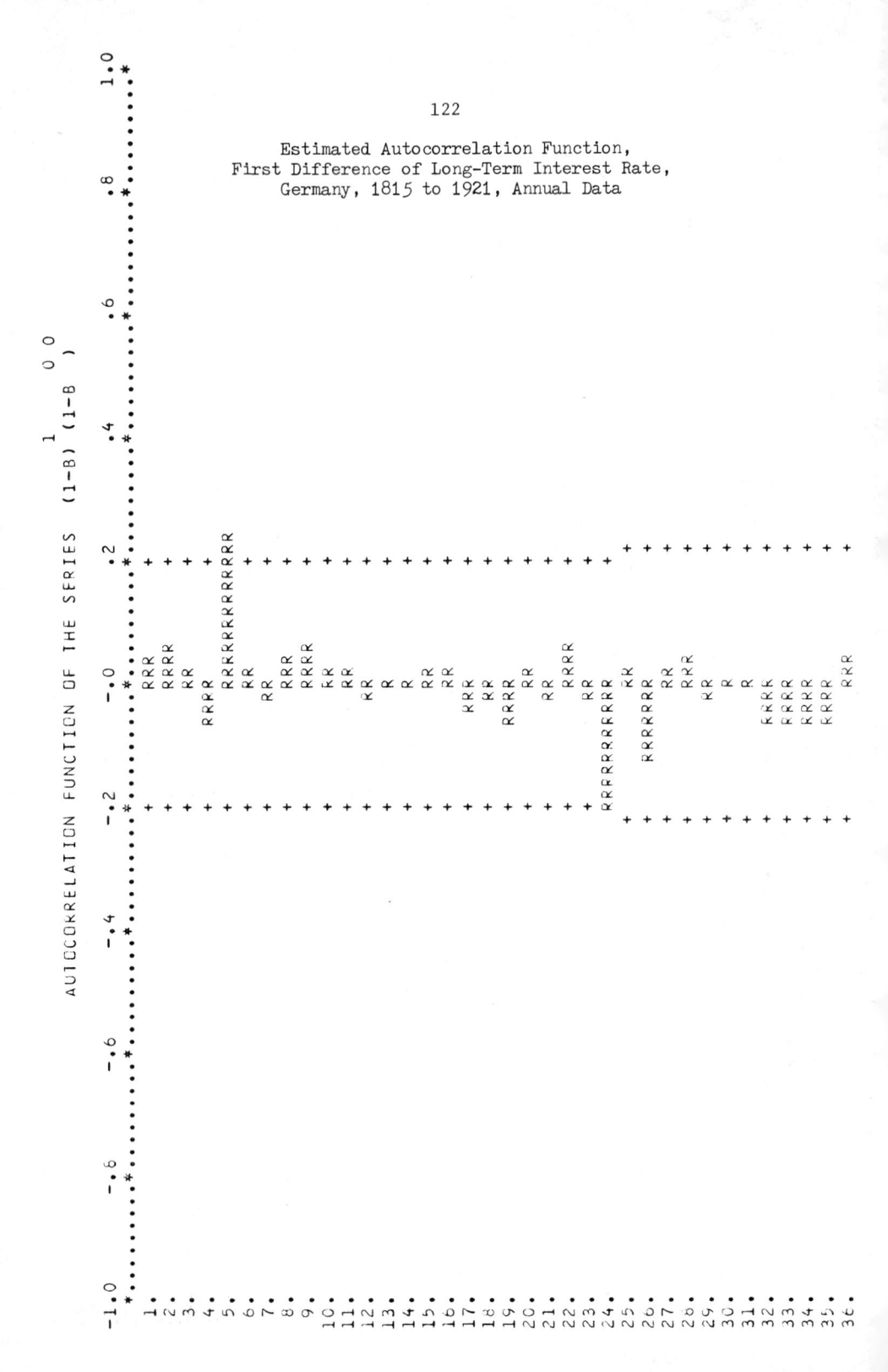

$(1-B)^1 (1-B)^0$

Estimated Partial Autocorrelation Function,
First Difference of Long-Term Interest Rate,
Germany, 1815 to 1921, Annual Data

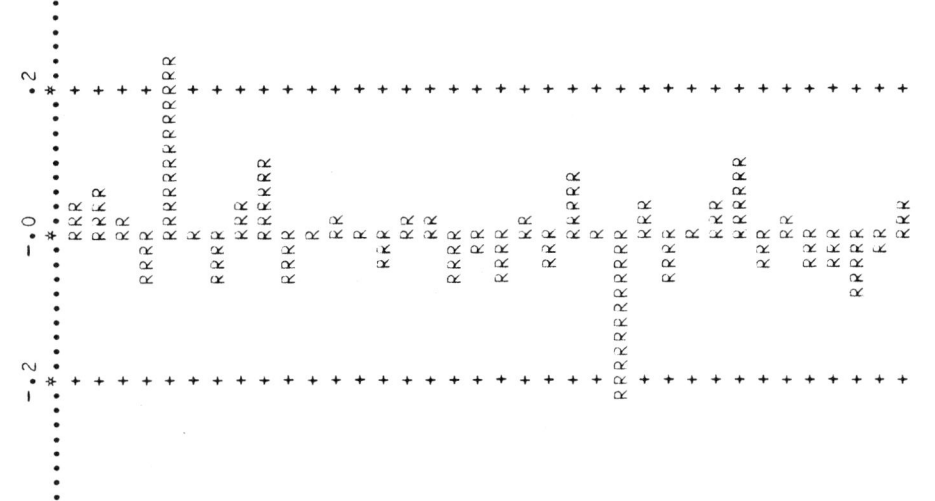

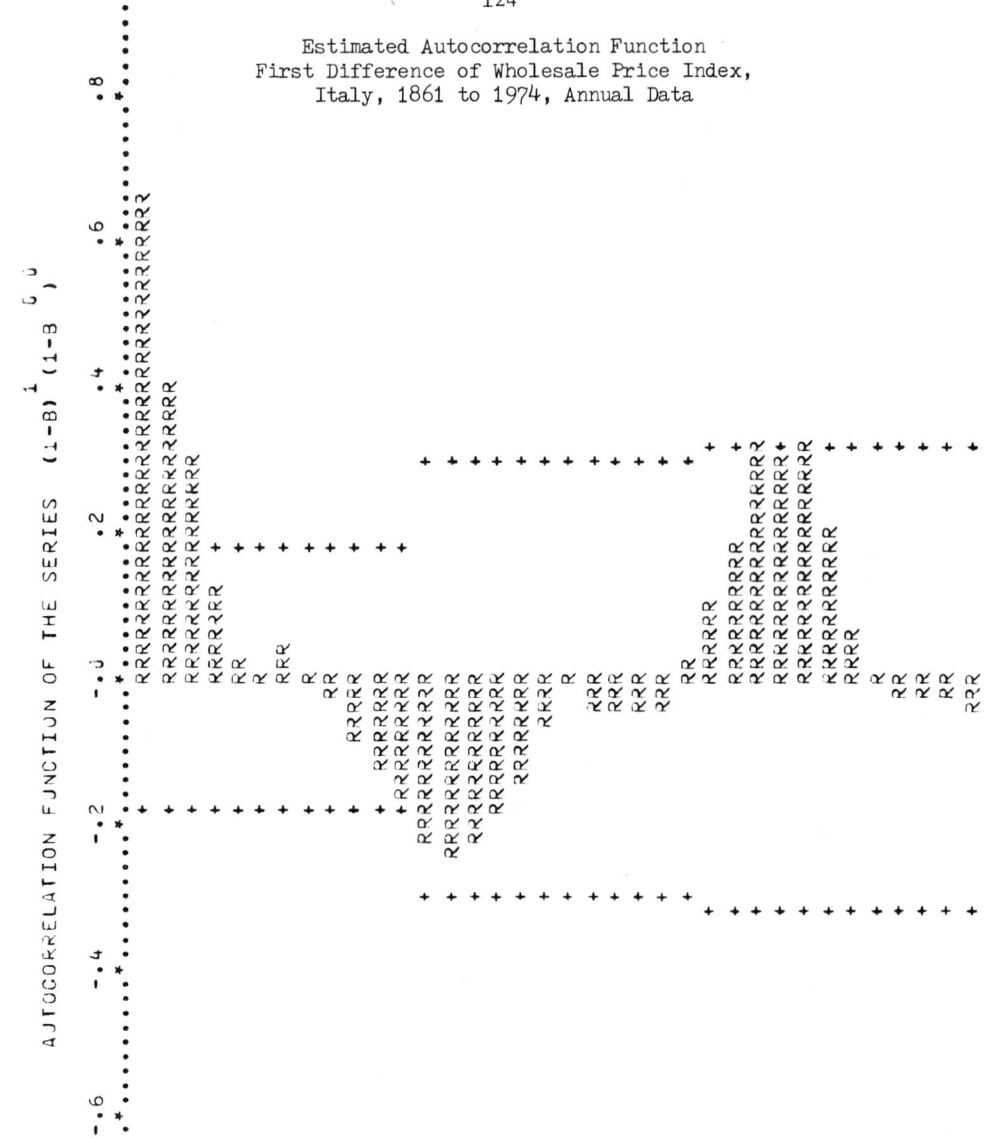

Estimated Autocorrelation Function
First Difference of Wholesale Price Index,
Italy, 1861 to 1974, Annual Data

125

Estimated Partial Autocorrelation Function
First Difference of Wholesale Price Index,
Italy, 1861 to 1974, Annual Data

Estimated Autocorrelation Function,
First Difference of Long-Term Interest Rate,
Italy, 1924 to 1974, Annual Data

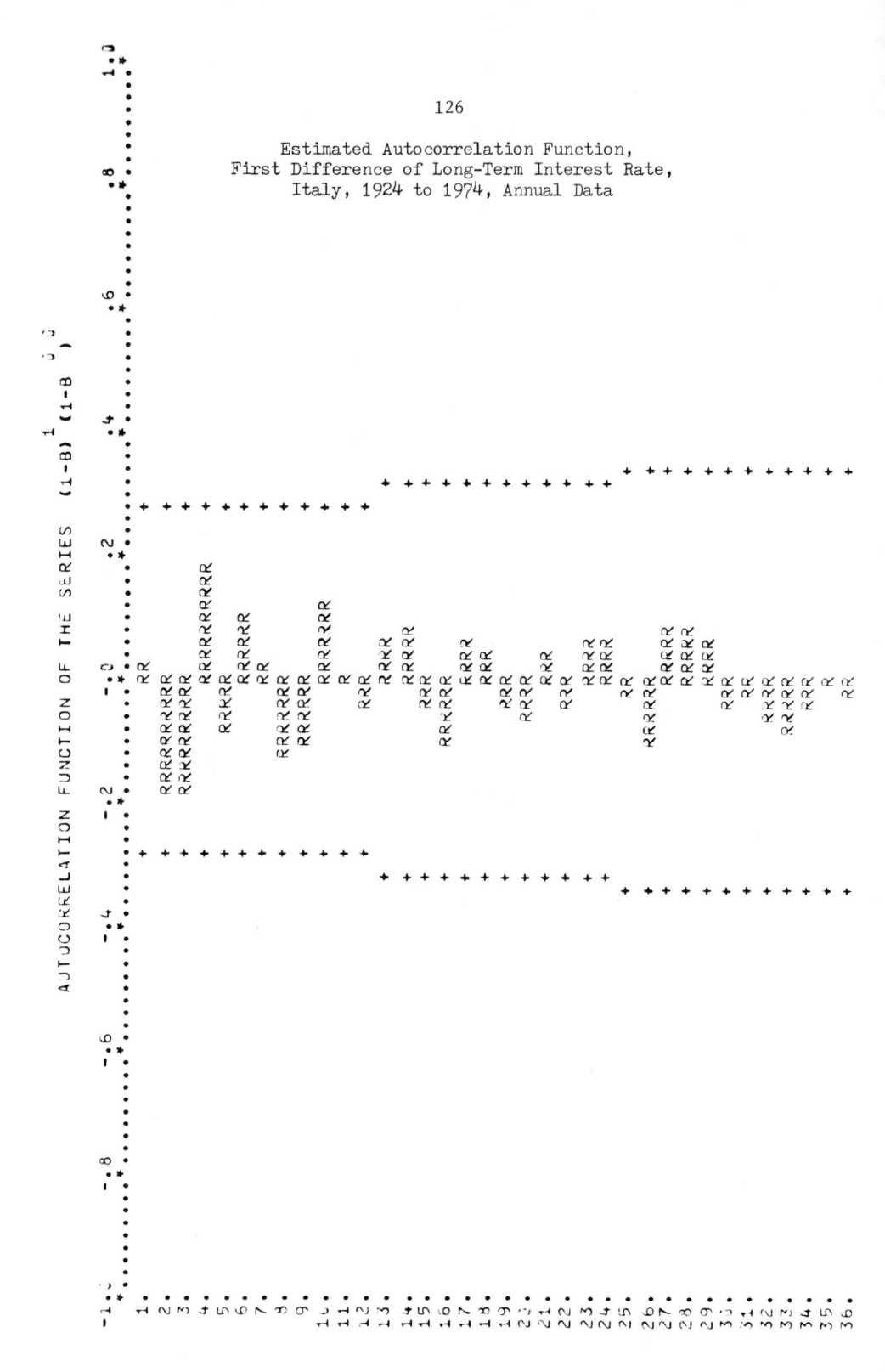

Estimated Partial Autocorrelation Function
First Difference of Long-Term Interest Rate,
Italy, 1924 to 1974, Annual Data

Estimated Autocorrelation Function,
First Difference of Wholesale Price Index,
Netherlands, 1901 to 1974, Annual Data

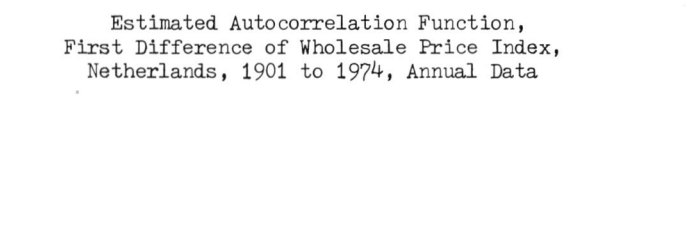

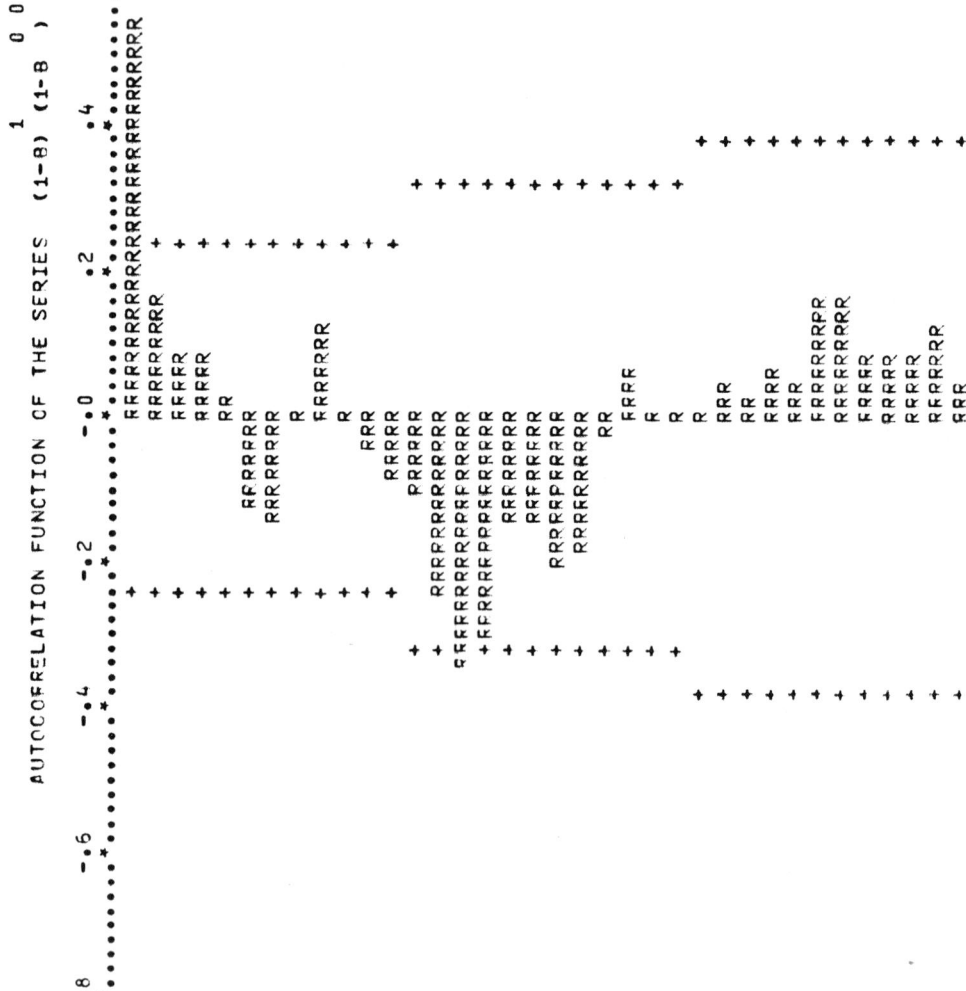

129

Estimated Partial Autocorrelation Function
First Difference of Wholesale Price Index,
Netherlands, 1901 to 1974, Annual Data

PARTIAL AUTOCORRELATION FUNCTION OF THE SERIES $(1-B)^1 (1-B^0)^0$

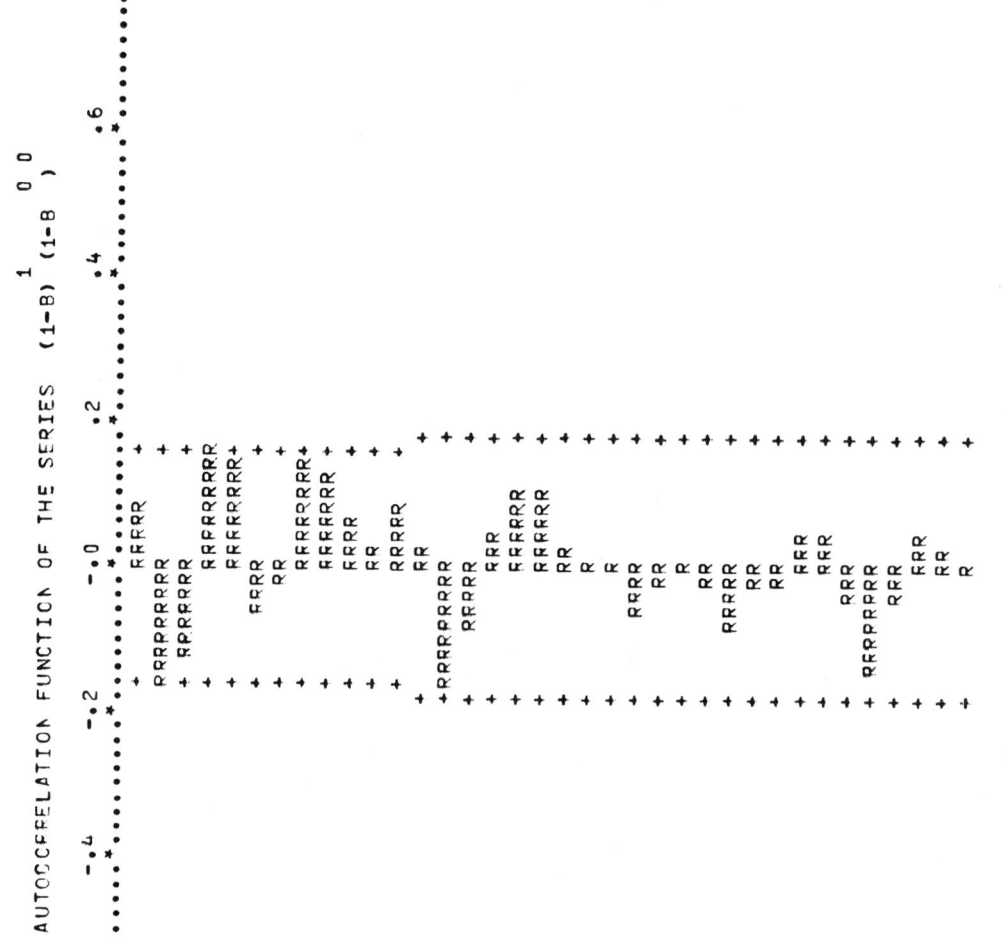

Estimated Autocorrelation Function,
First Difference of Long-Term Interest Rate,
Netherlands, 1814 to 1974, Annual Data

Estimated Partial Autocorrelation Function,
First Difference of Long-Term Interest Rate,
Netherlands, 1814 to 1974, Annual Data

Estimated Autocorrelation Function,
First Difference of Wholesale Price Index,
Switzerland, 1921 to 1974, Annual Data

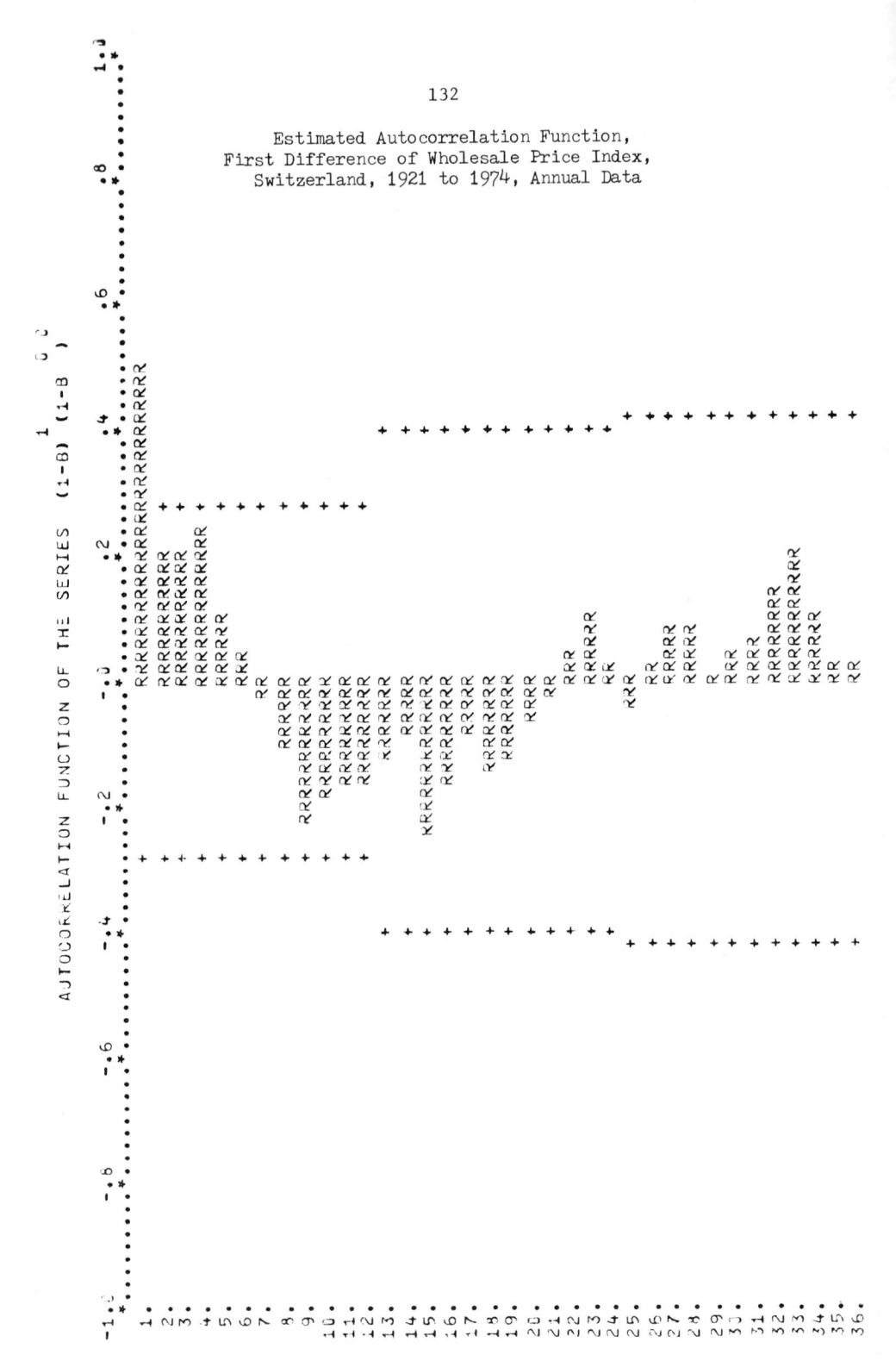

Estimated Partial Autocorrelation Function
First Difference of Wholesale Price Index,
Switzerland, 1921 to 1974, Annual Data

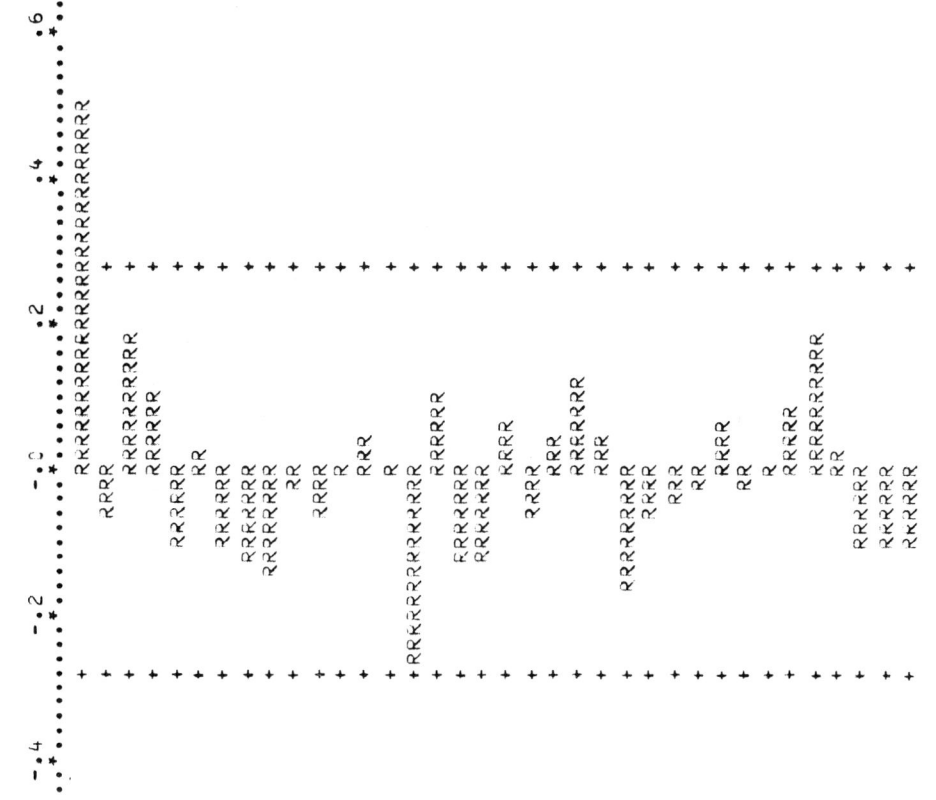

Estimated Autocorrelation Function,
First Difference of Long-Term Interest Rate,
Switzerland, 1916 to 1974, Annual Data

Estimated Partial Autocorrelation Function,
First Difference of Long-Term Interest Rate,
Switzerland, 1916 to 1974, Annual Data

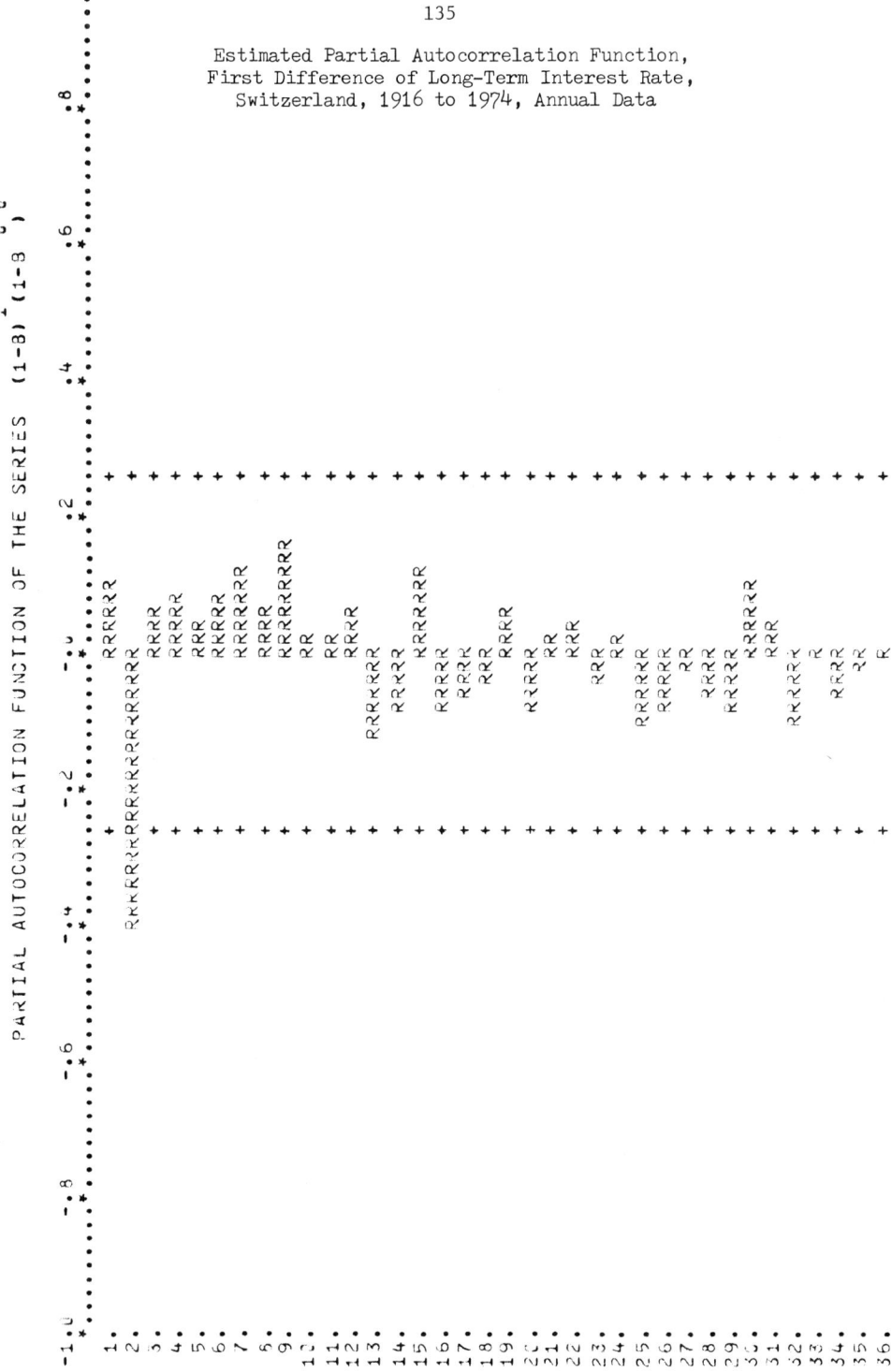

Estimated Autocorrelation Function,
First Difference of Wholesale Price Index,
United States, 1870 to 1974, Annual Data

Estimated Partial Autocorrelation Function,
First Difference of Wholesale Price Index,
United States, 1870 to 1974, Annual Data

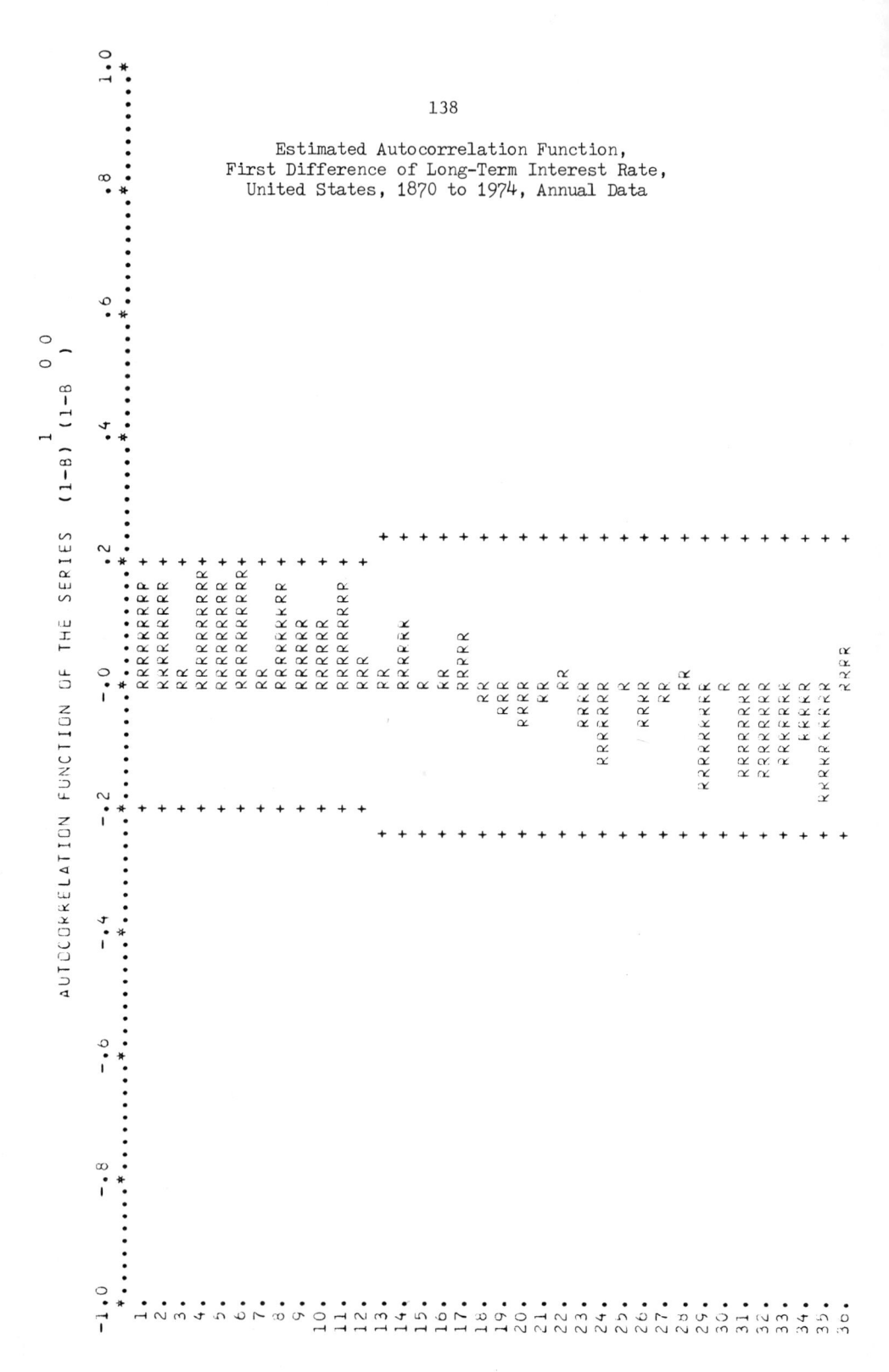

Estimated Autocorrelation Function,
First Difference of Long-Term Interest Rate,
United States, 1870 to 1974, Annual Data

139

Estimated Partial Autocorrelation Function,
First Difference of Long-Term Interest Rate,
United States, 1870 to 1974, Annual Data

APPENDIX B

Plots of Autocorrelation and Partial Autocorrelation Functions
Estimated from First Differences of
Real Gross National Product, the Implicit GNP Deflator,
The Long-Term Interest Rate, the Nominal Money Stock,
Government Purchases of Goods and Services,
and an Index of Full-Employment Output,
United States, 1890 to 1969, Annual Data

Note: Except for those pertaining to the Long-Term Interest Rate, all autocorrelation and partial autocorrelation functions were estimated using logarithmic data.

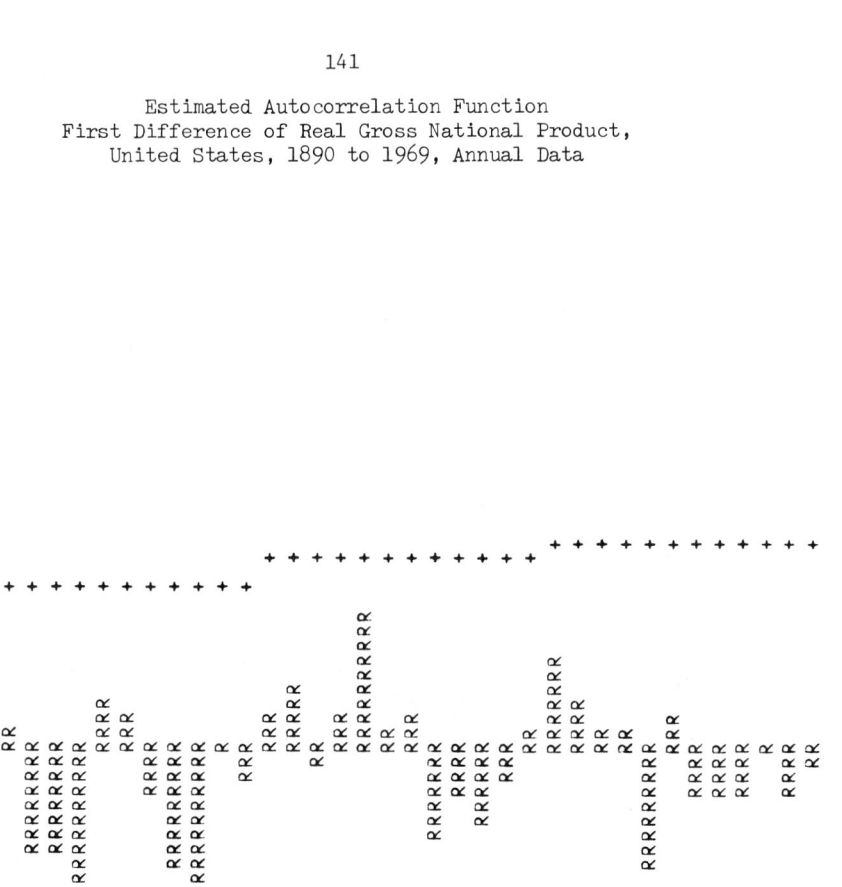

Estimated Autocorrelation Function
First Difference of Real Gross National Product,
United States, 1890 to 1969, Annual Data

Estimated Partial Autocorrelation Function
First Difference of Real Gross National Product,
United States, 1890 to 1969, Annual Data

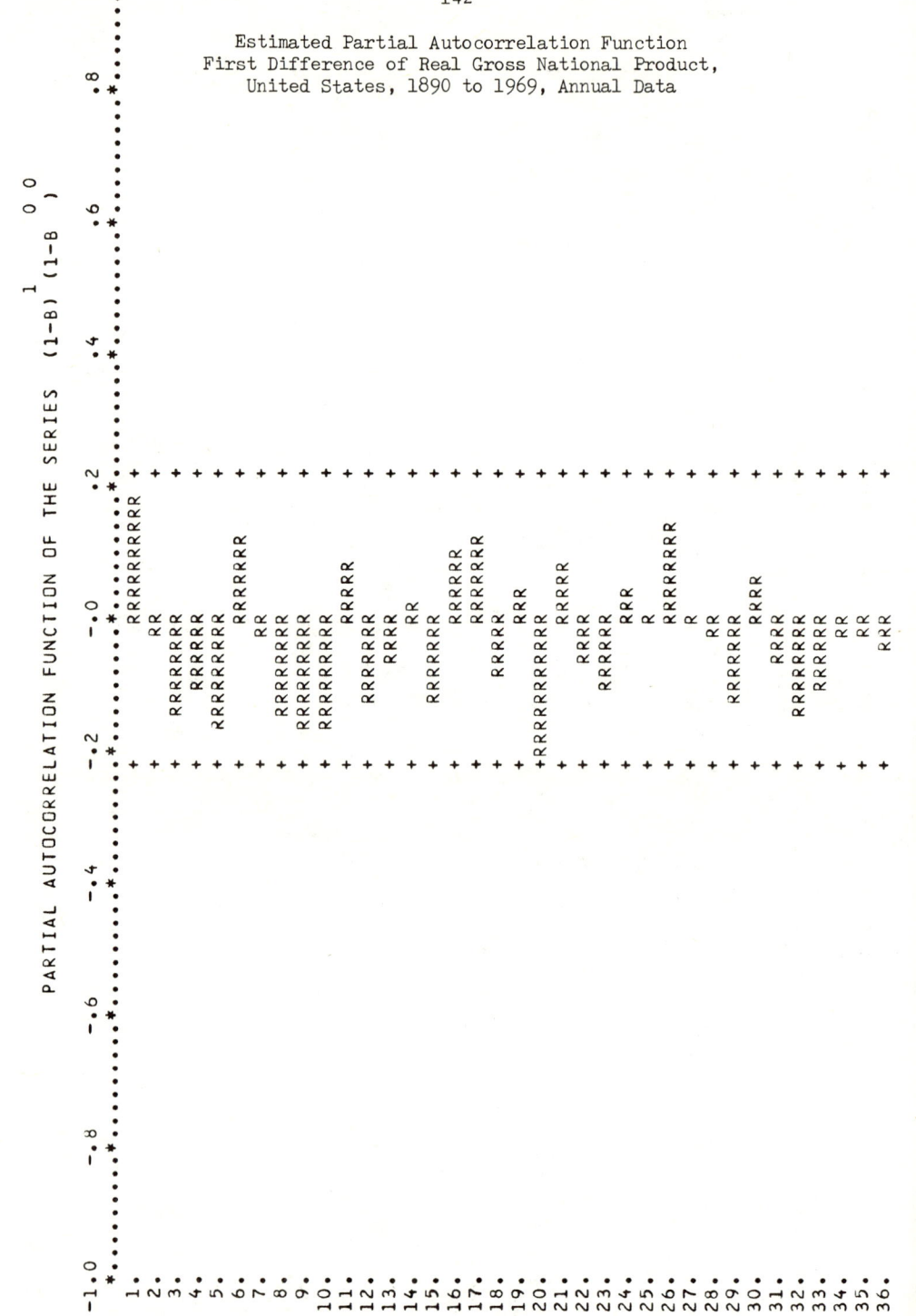

$$(1-B)^1 (1-B)^0$$

Estimated Autocorrelation Function,
First Difference of Implicit GNP Deflator,
United States, 1890 to 1969, Annual Data

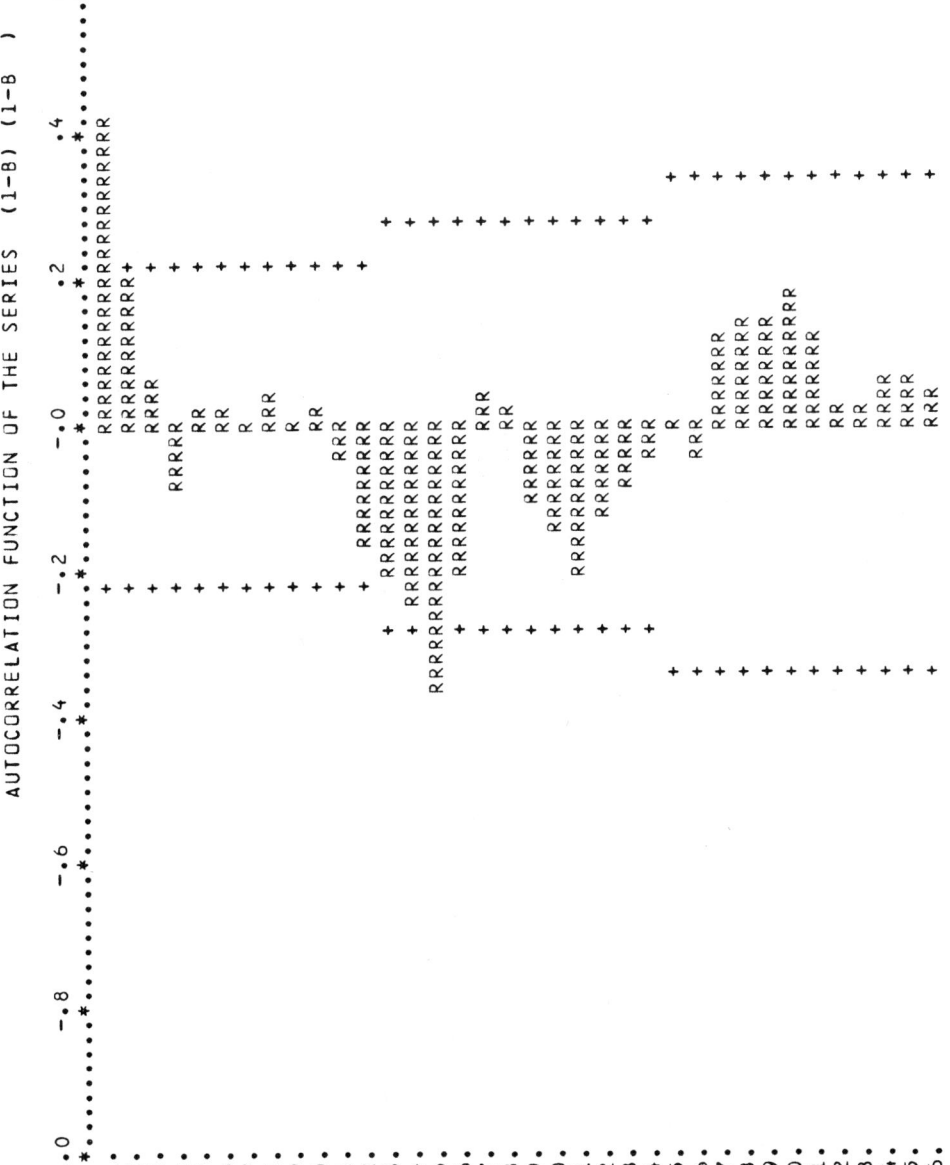

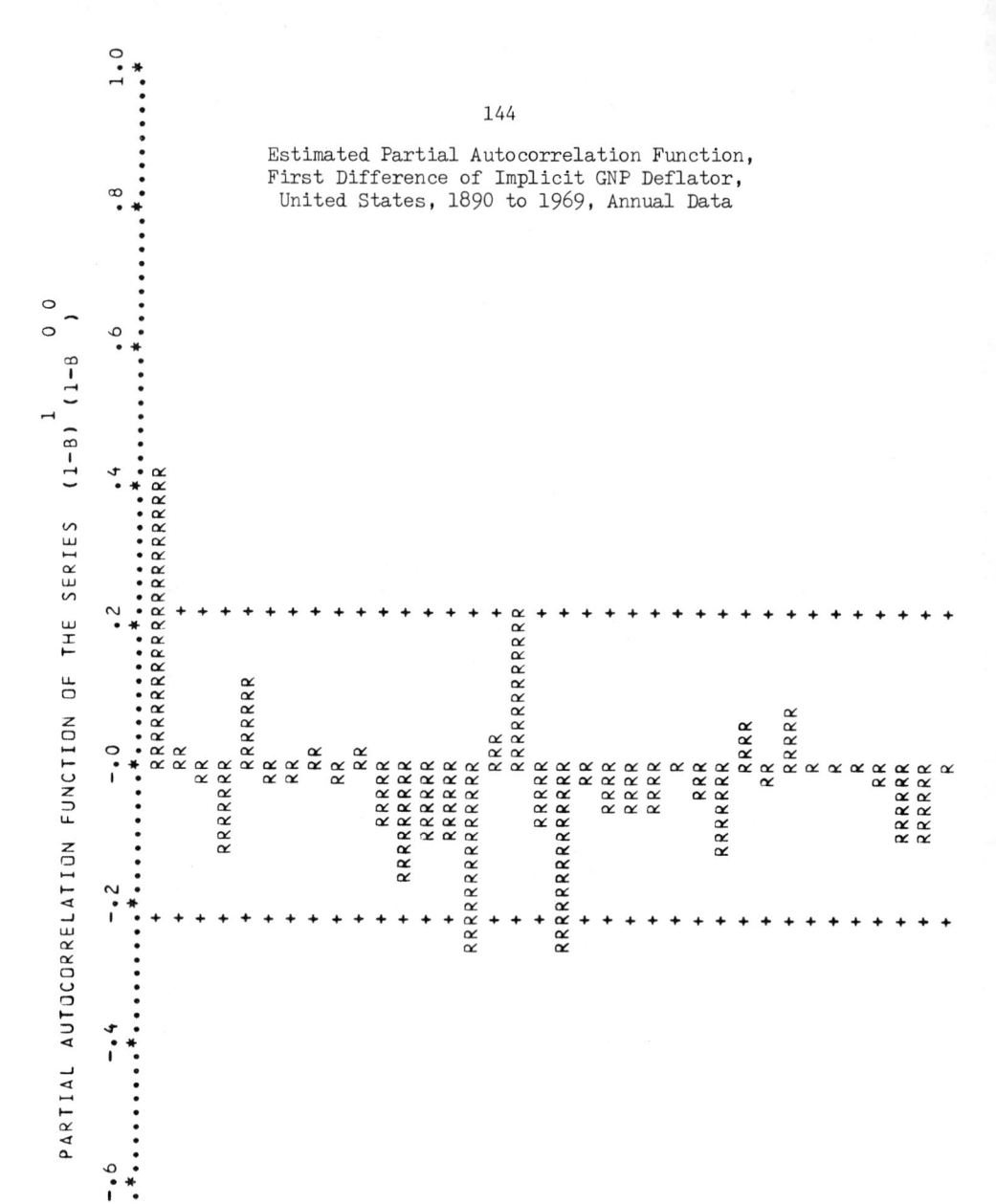

Estimated Partial Autocorrelation Function,
First Difference of Implicit GNP Deflator,
United States, 1890 to 1969, Annual Data

Estimated Autocorrelation Function,
First Difference of Long-Term Interest Rate,
United States, 1890 to 1969, Annual Data

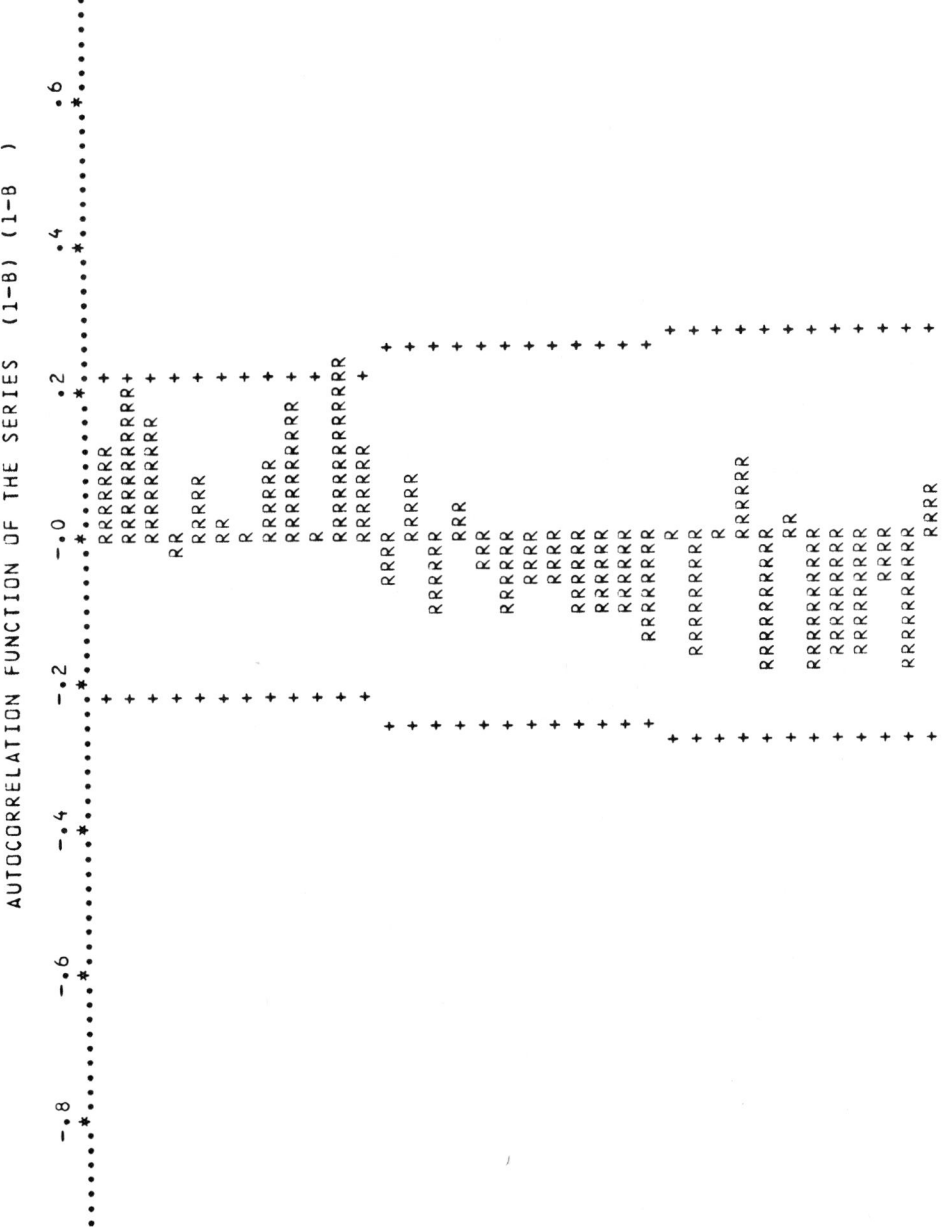

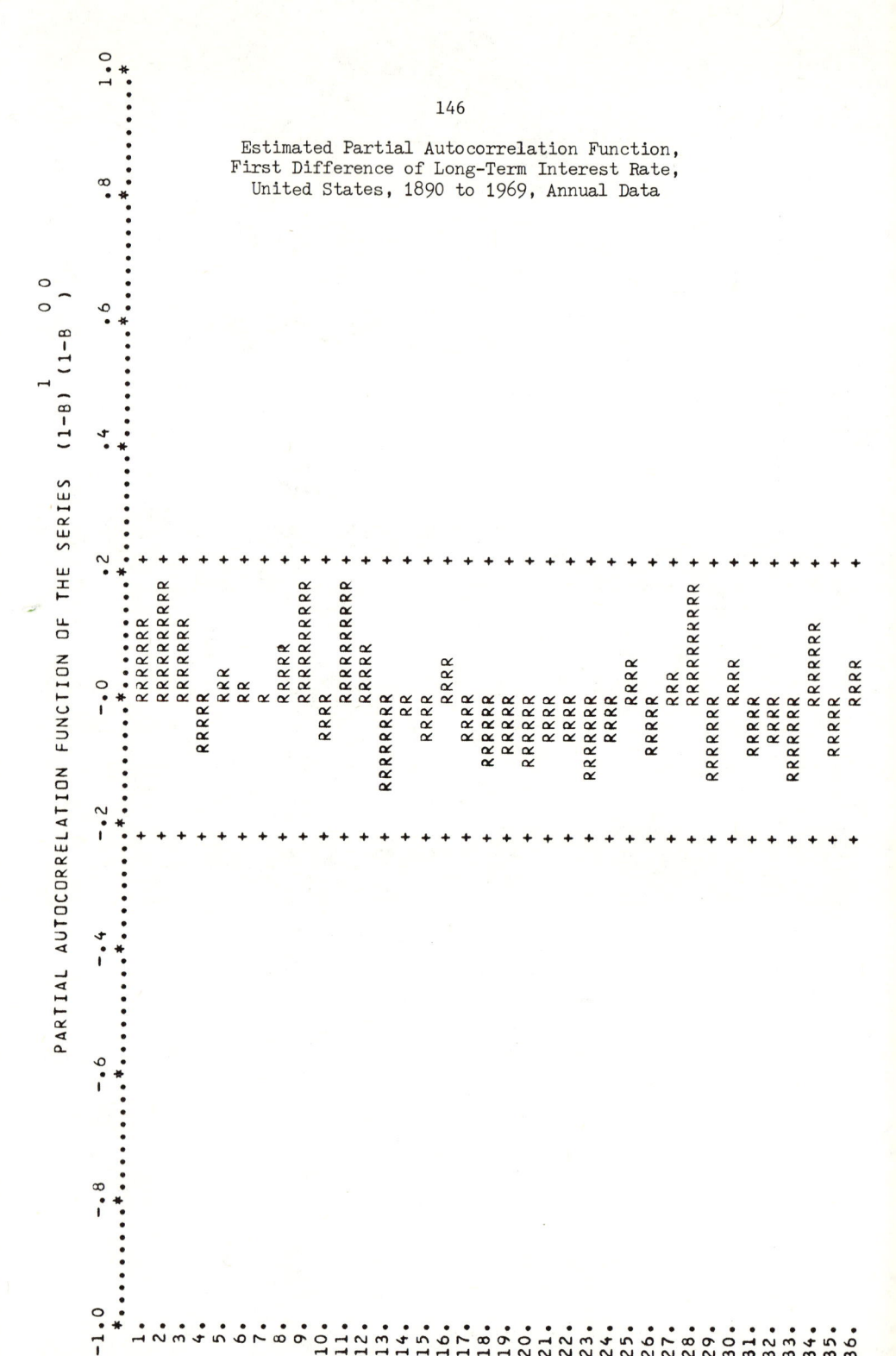

Estimated Partial Autocorrelation Function,
First Difference of Long-Term Interest Rate,
United States, 1890 to 1969, Annual Data

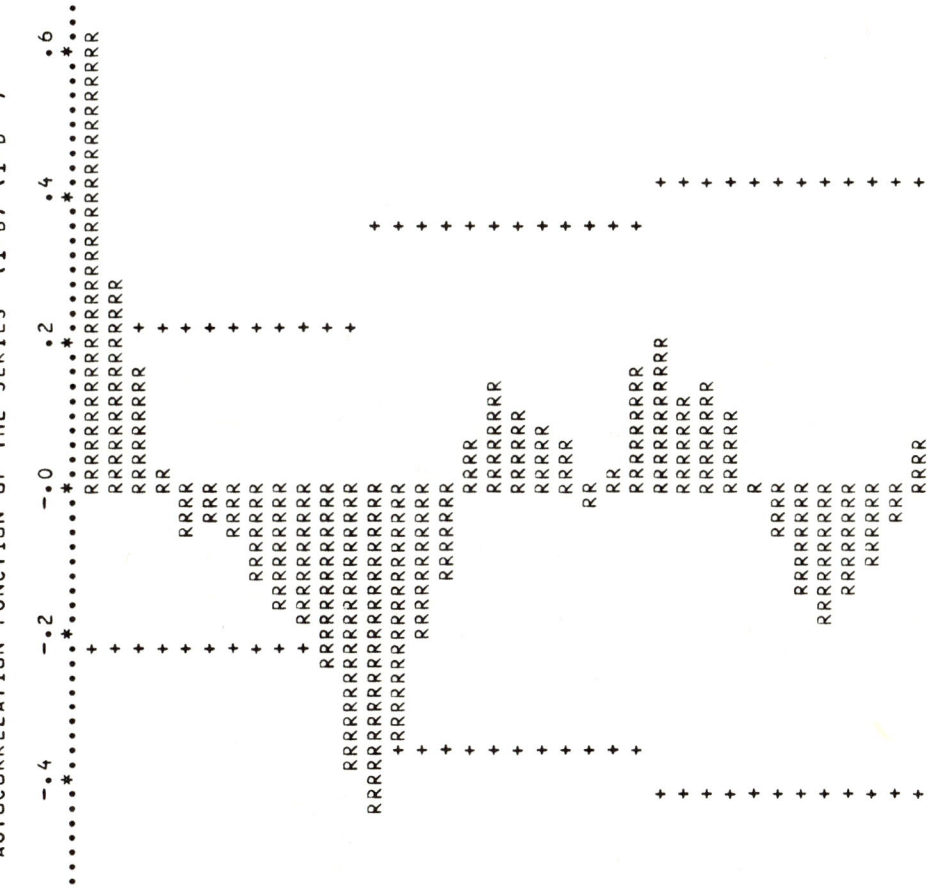

Estimated Autocorrelation Function,
First Difference of Nominal Money Stock,
United States, 1890 to 1969, Annual Data

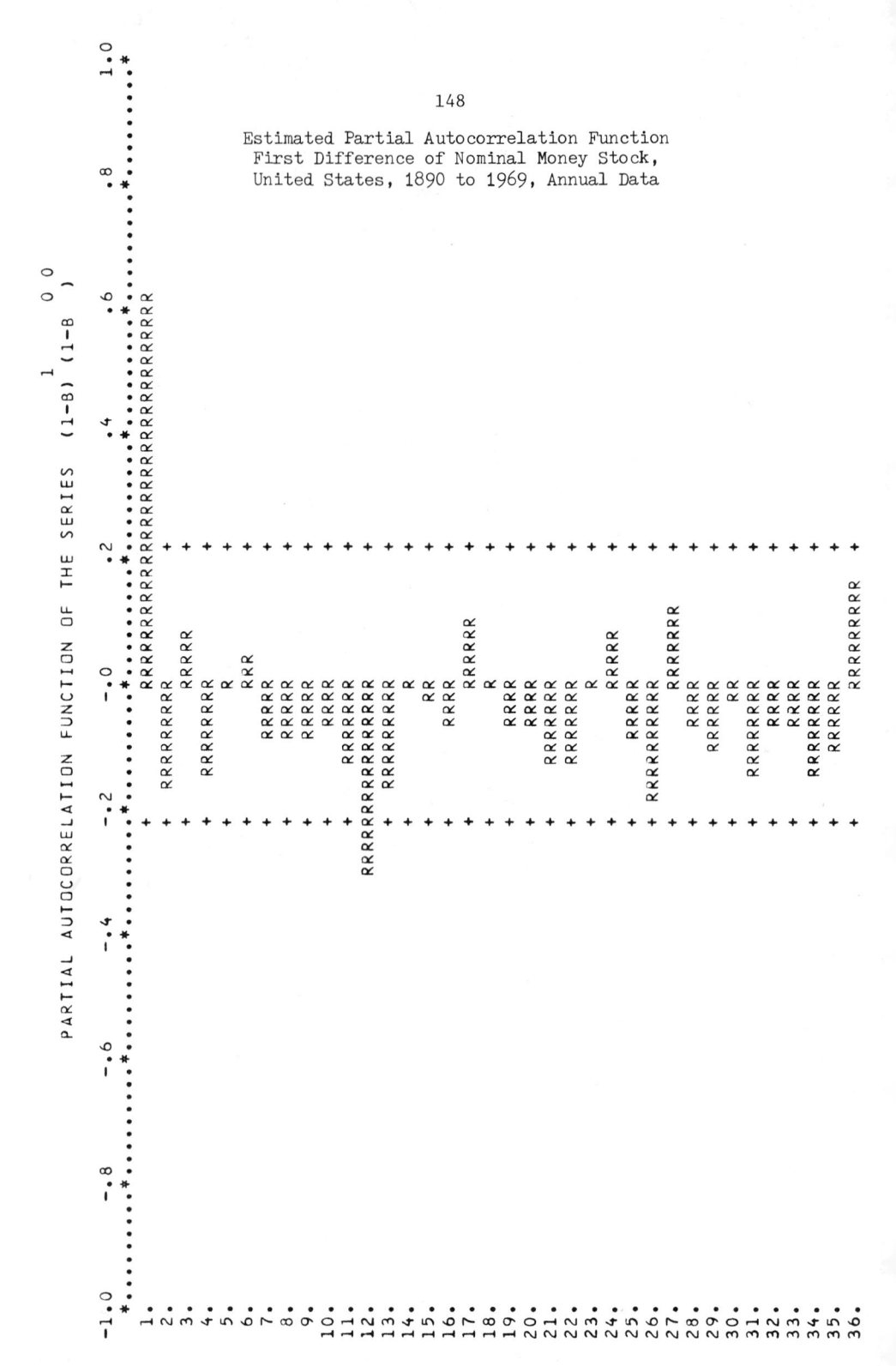

Estimated Partial Autocorrelation Function
First Difference of Nominal Money Stock,
United States, 1890 to 1969, Annual Data

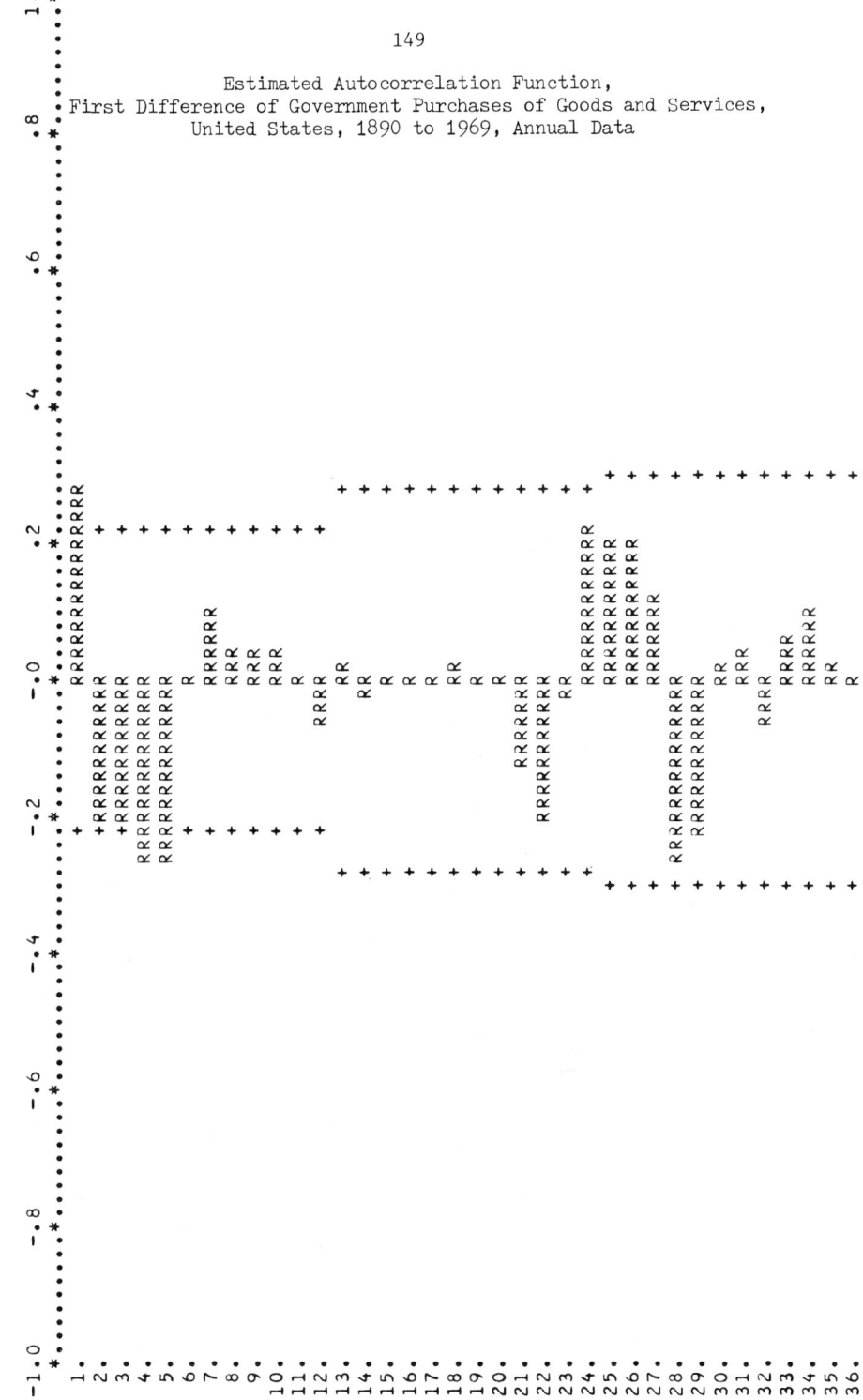

Estimated Autocorrelation Function,
First Difference of Government Purchases of Goods and Services,
United States, 1890 to 1969, Annual Data

$(1-B)^1 (1-B)^0$

Estimated Partial Autocorrelation Function,
First Difference of Government Purchases of Goods and Services,
United States, 1890 to 1969, Annual Data

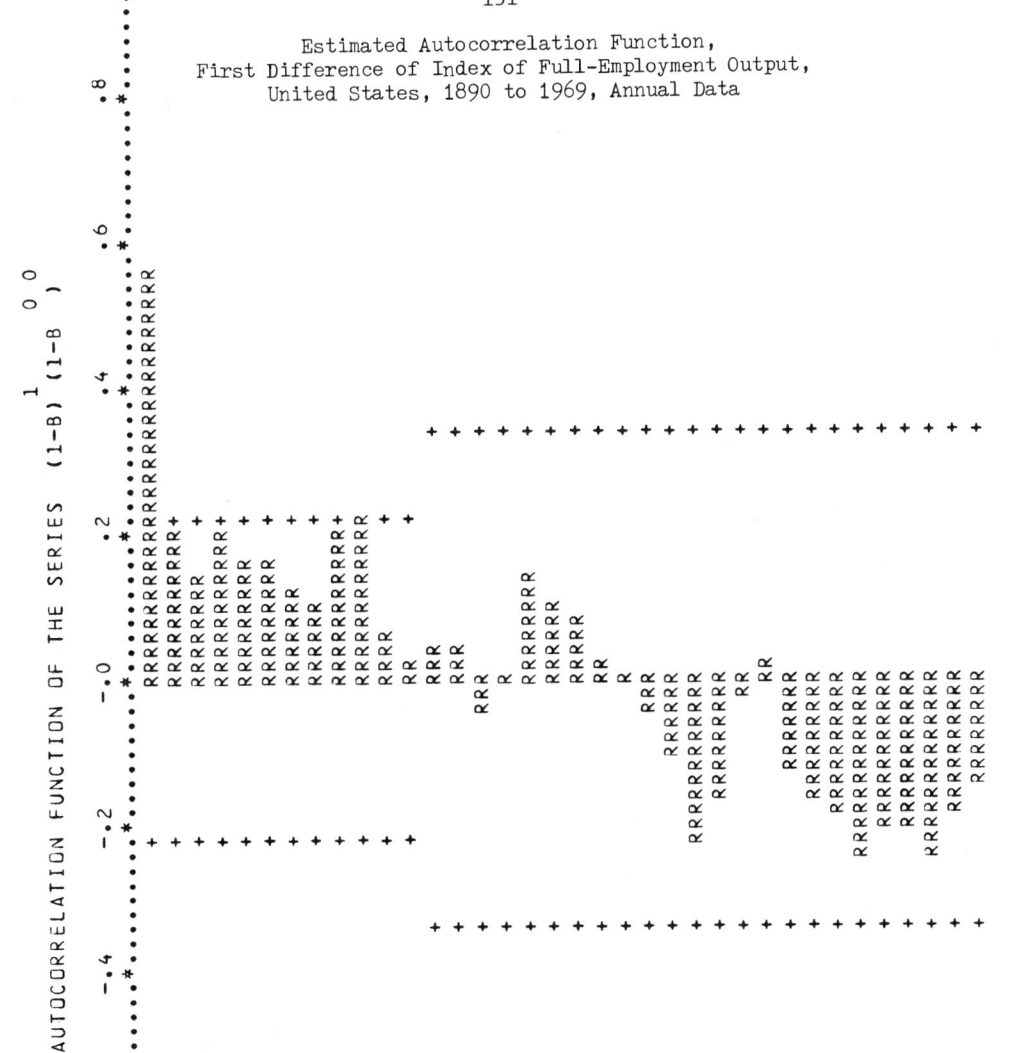

Estimated Autocorrelation Function,
First Difference of Index of Full-Employment Output,
United States, 1890 to 1969, Annual Data

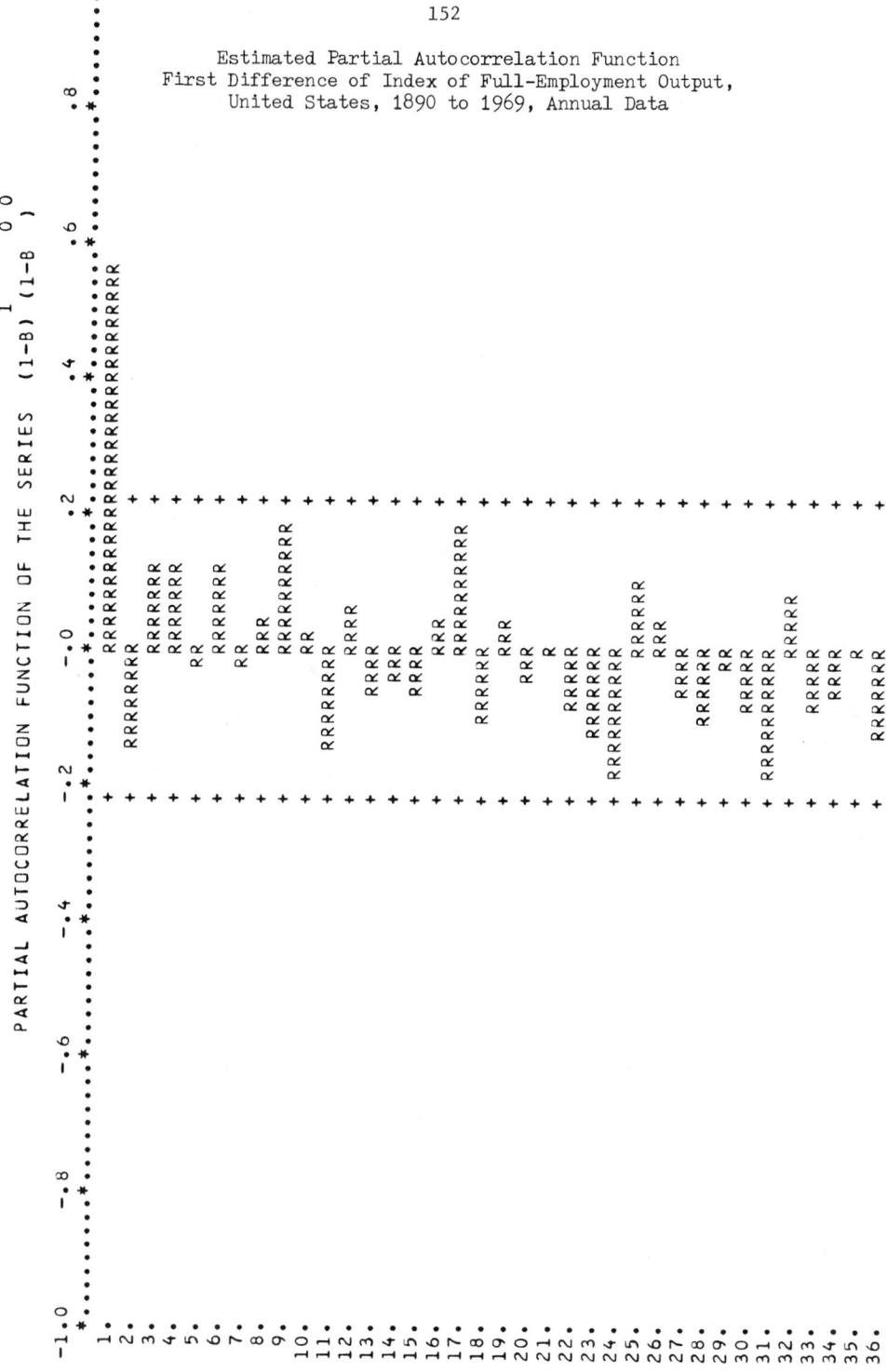

Estimated Partial Autocorrelation Function
First Difference of Index of Full-Employment Output,
United States, 1890 to 1969, Annual Data

APPENDIX C

Arima Models Fitted to the Logarithm of Real Gross National Product,
The Logarithm of the Implicit GNP Deflator, the Long-Term Interest Rate,
The Logarithm of the Nominal Money Stock,
The Logarithm of Nominal Government Purchases of Goods and Services,
and the Logarithm of an Index of Full-Employment Output,
United States, 1890 to 1969, Annual Data

ARIMA MODELS FITTED TO THE LOGARITHM OF REAL GROSS NATIONAL PRODUCT,
UNITED STATES, 1890 TO 1969, ANNUAL DATA

Time Series Process: ARIMA (1,1,0)
Fitted Model:

$$(1 - .19L) \Delta \log y_t = .027 + \hat{a}_{yt}$$
$$(1.70) \qquad\qquad\qquad (3.33)$$

$R^2 = .04$
D.F. = 77
$\hat{\sigma}^2 = .00397$

Box-Pierce Statistics	Degrees of Freedom	Critical Q Values (10% level of sig.)
Q(12) = 9.7	11	17.3
Q(24) = 15.6	23	32.0

Time Series Process: ARIMA (0,1,1)
Fitted Model:

$$\Delta \log y_t = .033 + (1 + .18L)\hat{a}_{yt}$$
$$\qquad\qquad (3.92) \qquad (1.60)$$

$R^2 = .04$
D.F. = 77
$\hat{\sigma}^2 = .00398$

Box-Pierce Statistics	Degrees of Freedom	Critical Q Values (10% level of sig.)
Q(12) = 9.9	11	17.3
Q(24) = 15.9	23	32.0

Note: 1. t-statistics are in parentheses.

2. L is a lag operator such that $L^n x_t = x_{t-n}$.

3. Q(K) is distributed χ^2 with K - p - q degrees of freedom, where p + q equals the number of autoregressive and moving average parameters estimated.

Sources: See Data Appendix.

ARIMA MODELS FITTED TO THE LOGARITHM OF THE IMPLICIT GNP DEFLATOR, UNITED STATES, 1890 TO 1969, ANNUAL DATA

Time Series Process: ARIMA (0,1,0)
Fitted Model:

$$\Delta \log P_t = \underset{(3.46)}{.020} + \hat{a}_{Pt}$$

D.F. = 78
$\hat{\sigma}^2$ = .00276

Box-Pierce Statistics	Degrees of Freedom	Critical Q Values (10% level of sig.)
Q(12) = 21.2	12	18.5
Q(24) = 50.0	24	33.2

Time Series Process: ARIMA (0,1,1)
Fitted Model:

$$\Delta \log P_t = \underset{(2.72)}{.021} + \underset{(3.70)}{(1 + .39L)}\hat{a}_{Pt}$$

R^2 = .16
D.F. = 77
$\hat{\sigma}^2$ = .00236

Box-Pierce Statistics	Degrees of Freedom	Critical Q Values (10% level of sig.)
Q(12) = 5.7	11	17.3
Q(24) = 20.2	23	32.0

Time Series Process: ARIMA (1,1,1)
Fitted Model:

$$\underset{(1.96)}{(1 - .46L)} \Delta \log P_t = \underset{(1.58)}{.011} + \underset{(.14)}{(1 - .036L)}\hat{a}_{Pt}$$

R^2 = .18
D.F. = 76
$\hat{\sigma}^2$ = .00231

Box-Pierce Statistics	Degrees of Freedom	Critical Q Values (10% level of sig.)
Q(12) = 4.3	10	16.0
Q(24) = 17.9	22	30.8

Time Series Process: (2,1,1)
Fitted Model:

$$\underset{(3.69)\quad(.16)}{(1 - .42L - .018L^2)} \Delta \log P_t = \underset{(1.94)}{.011} + \hat{a}_{Pt}$$

R^2 = .18
D.F. = 76
$\hat{\sigma}^2$ = .00231

Box-Pierce Statistics	Degrees of Freedom	Critical Q Values (10% level of sig.)
Q(12) = 4.3	10	16.0
Q(24) = 17.9	22	30.8

Note: 1. t-statistics are in parentheses.
2. L is a lag operator such that $L^n x_t = x_{t-n}$.
3. Q(K) is distributed χ^2 with K - p - q degrees of freedom, where p + q equals the number of autoregressive and moving average parameters estimated.

Sources: See Data Appendix.

ARIMA MODELS FITTED TO THE LONG-TERM INTEREST RATE, UNITED STATES, 1890 TO 1969, ANNUAL DATA

Time Series Process: ARIMA (1,1,0)
Fitted Model:

$$(1 - .12L) \Delta R_t = .00032 + \hat{a}_{Rt}$$
$$(1.02)(1.07)$$

$R^2 = .01$
D.F. = 77
$\hat{\sigma}^2 = .00000701$

Box-Pierce Statistics	Degrees of Freedom	Critical Q Values (10% level of sig.)
Q(12) = 13.4	11	17.3
Q(24) = 19.3	23	32.0

Time Series Process: ARIMA (0,1,1)
Fitted Model:

$$\Delta R_t = .00035 + (1 + .085L)\hat{a}_{Rt}$$
$$(1.10)(.74)$$

$R^2 = .01$
D.F. = 77
$\hat{\sigma}^2 = .00000704$

Box-Pierce Statistics	Degrees of Freedom	Critical Q Values (10% level of sig.)
Q(12) = 13.4	11	17.3
Q(24) = 19.6	23	32.0

Note: 1. t-statistics are in parentheses.
2. L is a lag operator such that $L^n x_t = x_{t-n}$.
3. Q(K) is distributed χ^2 with K - p - q degrees of freedom, where p + q equals the number of autoregressive and moving average parameters estimated.

Sources: See Data Appendix.

ARIMA MODELS FITTED TO THE LOGARITHM OF THE NOMINAL MONEY STOCK
UNITED STATES, 1890 TO 1969, ANNUAL DATA

Time Series Process: ARIMA (1,1,0)
Fitted Model:

$$(1 - .61L) \Delta \log M_t = .022 + \hat{a}_{Mt}$$
$$(6.82)(2.95)$$

$R^2 = .38$
D.F. = 77
$\hat{\sigma}^2 = .00250$

Box-Pierce Statistics	Degrees of Freedom	Critical Q Values (10% level of sig.)
Q(12) = 6.7	11	17.3
Q(24) = 20.1	23	32.0

Time Series Process: ARIMA (0,1,1)
Fitted Model:

$$\Delta \log M_t = .058 + (1 + .63L)\hat{a}_{Mt}$$
$$(6.30)(7.30)$$

$R^2 = .36$
D.F. = 77
$\hat{\sigma}^2 = .00254$

Box-Pierce Statistics	Degrees of Freedom	Critical Q Values (10% level of sig.)
Q(12) = 14.6	11	17.3
Q(24) = 30.0	23	32.0

Time Series Process: ARIMA (2,1,1)
Fitted Model:

$$(1 - .17L - .16L^2)\Delta \log M_t = .039 + (1 + .58L)\hat{a}_{Mt}$$
$$(.44)(.58)(2.85)(1.64)$$

$R^2 = .40$
D.F. = 75
$\hat{\sigma}^2 = .00245$

Box-Pierce Statistics	Degrees of Freedom	Critical Q Values (10% level of sig.)
Q(12) = 4.1	9	14.7
Q(24) = 14.8	21	29.6

Time Series Process: ARIMA (1,1,2)
Fitted Model:

$$(1 - .56L) \Delta \log M_t = .026 + (1 + .19L - .14L^2)\hat{a}_{Mt}$$
$$(1.57)(1.20)(.50)(.49)$$

$R^2 = .40$
D.F. = 75
$\hat{\sigma}^2 = .00245$

Box-Pierce Statistics	Degrees of Freedom	Critical Q Values (10% level of sig.)
Q(12) = 4.0	9	14.7
Q(24) = 14.5	21	29.6

Note: 1. t-statistics are in parentheses.
2. L is a lag operator such that $L^n x_t = x_{t-n}$.
3. $Q(K)$ is distributed χ^2 with $K - p - q$ degrees of freedom, where $p + q$ equals the number of autoregressive and moving average parameters estimated.

Sources: See Data Appendix.

ARIMA MODELS FITTED TO THE LOGARITHM OF
NOMINAL GOVERNMENT PURCHASES OF GOODS AND SERVICES,
UNITED STATES, 1890 TO 1969, ANNUAL DATA

Time Series Process: ARIMA (1,1,0)
Fitted Model:

$$(1 - .28L) \Delta \log G_t = .053 + \hat{a}_{Gt}$$
$$(2.52)(1.84)$$

$R^2 = .08$

D.F. = 77

$\hat{\sigma}^2 = .0599$

Box-Pierce Statistics	Degrees of Freedom	Critical Q Values (10% level of sig.)
Q(12) = 14.5	11	17.3
Q(24) = 21.5	23	32.0

Time Series Process: ARIMA (1,1,1)
Fitted Model:

$$(1 - .18L) \Delta \log G_t = .086 + (1 + .58L)\hat{a}_{Gt}$$
$$(.71)(1.87)(2.79)$$

$R^2 = .14$

D.F. = 76

$\hat{\sigma}^2 = .0565$

Box-Pierce Statistics	Degrees of Freedom	Critical Q Values (10% level of sig.)
Q(12) = 9.9	10	16.0
Q(24) = 16.3	22	30.8

Time Series Process: ARIMA (0,1,2)
Fitted Model:

$$\Delta \log G_t = .073 + (1 + .33L - .17L^2)\hat{a}_{Gt}$$
$$(2.37)(2.92)(1.54)$$

$R^2 = .15$

D.F. = 76

$\hat{\sigma}^2 = .0559$

Box-Pierce Statistics	Degrees of Freedom	Critical Q Values (10% level of sig.)
Q(12) = 11.4	10	16.0
Q(24) = 17.7	22	30.8

Note: 1. t-statistics are in parentheses.
2. L is a lag operator such that $L^n x_t = x_{t-n}$.
3. Q(K) is distributed χ^2 with K - p - q degrees of freedom, where p + q equals the number of autoregressive and moving average parameters estimated.

Sources: See Data Appendix.

ARIMA MODELS FITTED TO THE LOGARITHM OF AN INDEX OF FULL-EMPLOYMENT OUTPUT, UNITED STATES, 1890 TO 1969, ANNUAL DATA

Time Series Process: ARIMA (0,1,1)
Fitted Model:

$$\Delta \log k_t = \underset{(11.32)}{.020} + \underset{(5.50)}{(1 + .53L)} \hat{a}_{kt}$$

$R^2 = .29$
D.F. = 77
$\hat{\sigma}^2 = .000101$

Box-Pierce Statistics	Degrees of Freedom	Critical Q Values (10% level of sig.)
Q(12) = 14.3	11	17.3
Q(24) = 20.3	23	32.0

Time Series Process: ARIMA (1,1,1)
Fitted Model:

$$\underset{(2.13)}{(1 - .38L)} \Delta \log k_t = \underset{(3.27)}{.012} + \underset{(1.51)}{(1 + .28L)} \hat{a}_{kt}$$

$R^2 = .33$
D.F. = 76
$\hat{\sigma}^2 = .0000969$

Box-Pierce Statistics	Degrees of Freedom	Critical Q Values (10% level of sig.)
Q(12) = 8.4	10	16.0
Q(24) = 14.0	22	30.8

Time Series Process: ARIMA (2,1,0)
Fitted Model:

$$\underset{(5.64)\quad(1.23)}{(1 - .64L + .14L^2)} \Delta \log k_t = \underset{(4.21)}{.0098} + \hat{a}_{kt}$$

$R^2 = .33$
D.F. = 76
$\hat{\sigma}^2 = .0000976$

Box-Pierce Statistics	Degrees of Freedom	Critical Q Values (10% level of sig.)
Q(12) = 9.4	10	16.0
Q(24) = 15.0	22	30.8

Note:
1. t-statistics are in parentheses.
2. L is a lag operator such that $L^n x_t = x_{t-n}$.
3. Q(K) is distributed χ^2 with K - p - q degrees of freedom, where p + q equals the number of autoregressive and moving average parameters estimated.

Sources: See Data Appendix.

DATA APPENDIX

BELGIUM
WHOLESALE PRICE INDEX, 1832 TO 1913
1913 = 100

1832	79	1853	89	1874	102	1895	74
33	77	54	97	75	100	96	75
34	77	55	100	76	98	97	75
35	81	56	101	77	98	98	76
36	85	57	99	78	92	99	82
37	84	58	97	79	91		
38	87	59	91			1900	87
39	91			1880	98	01	86
		1860	94	81	99	02	84
1840	91	61	97	82	98	03	83
41	92	62	96	83	96	04	86
42	89	63	93	84	93	05	88
43	82	64	96	85	86	06	95
44	77	65	94	86	81	07	96
45	79	66	95	87	81	08	96
46	87	67	95	88	83	09	90
47	96	68	93	89	84		
48	80	69	93			1910	95
49	77			1890	86	11	96
		1870	94	91	86	12	100
1850	83	71	98	92	82	13	100
51	80	72	102	93	80		
52	75	73	103	94	78		

Source: Mitchell, B. R., 1975, European Historical Statistics 1750-1970 (The Macmillan Press LTD, London).

BELGIUM
LONG-TERM GOVERNMENT BOND YIELD
1831 TO 1913

Year	Yield	Year	Yield	Year	Yield	Year	Yield
1831	6.49	1852	4.64	1873	3.87	1894	2.56
32	5.86	53	4.52	74	4.08	95	2.57
33	5.37	54	4.98	75	4.08	96	2.65
34	4.85	55	4.70	76	4.08	97	2.63
35	4.64	56	4.60	77	3.98	98	2.62
36	4.68	57	4.48	78	3.97	99	2.78
37	4.70	58	4.48	79	3.81		
38	4.59	59	4.51			1900	2.92
39	4.64			1880	3.65	01	2.91
		1860	4.49	81	3.56	02	2.84
1840	4.46	61	4.42	82	3.56	03	2.77
41	4.76	62	4.37	83	3.58	04	2.85
42	4.75	63	4.10	84	3.56	05	2.88
43	4.51	64	4.26	85	3.40	06	2.92
44	4.20	65	4.25	86	3.13	07	3.03
45	4.17	66	4.36	87	3.12	08	3.14
46	4.45	67	4.43	88	3.10	09	3.11
47	4.76	68	4.23	89	3.11		
48	7.15	69	4.02			1910	3.22
49	5.47			1890	2.97	11	3.25
		1870	4.02	91	2.83	12	3.50
1850	5.05	71	4.04	92	2.82	13	3.92
51	4.97	72	3.91	93	2.69		

Source: Homer, S., 1963, *A History of Interest Rates* (Rutgers University Press, New Brunswick).

Note: Interest rate is the average annual yield on 2-1/2% Rentes.

CANADA
WHOLESALE PRICE INDEX, 1867 TO 1974
1935-1939 = 100

1867	80.2	1894	59.1	1921	143.4	1949	201.7
68	80.0	95	57.9	22	126.8		
69	80.7	96	55.9	23	127.7	1950	215.4
		97	56.8	24	129.5	51	246.3
1870	79.8	98	59.4	25	133.8	52	232.0
71	81.3	99	60.6	26	130.3	53	226.3
72	90.6			27	127.3	54	222.7
73	90.9	1900	62.4	28	125.6	55	226.0
74	86.4	01	63.7	29	124.6	56	233.7
75	82.8	02	66.6			57	233.8
76	77.6	03	67.5	1930	112.9	58	233.5
77	73.4	04	68.3	31	94.0	59	237.0
78	68.0	05	70.4	32	86.9		
79	65.5	06	70.7	33	87.4	1960	235.8
		07	76.4	34	93.4	61	237.9
1880	71.8	08	76.3	35	94.1	62	245.6
81	72.4	09	77.6	36	96.7	63	250.5
82	72.5			37	108.4	64	250.5
83	70.2	1910	78.5	38	101.9	65	256.6
84	67.0	11	81.1	39	99.0	66	265.7
85	63.3	12	85.2			67	270.6
86	62.3	13	83.4	1940	107.8	68	276.2
87	63.7	14	85.4	41	116.2	69	289.1
88	66.2	15	91.8	42	122.8		
89	66.1	16	109.8	43	127.8	1970	293.0
		17	148.9	44	130.5	71	296.5
1890	67.1	18	166.0	45	132.0	72	317.3
91	67.1	19	174.7	46	139.2	73	385.7
92	62.3			47	165.8	74	471.0
93	63.2	1920	203.2	48	197.2		

Sources: 1867-1959 from Urquhart, M.C. and Buckley, K.A.H. (eds.), 1965, Historical Statistics of Canada (Cambridge University Press, Cambridge).
1960-1974 from International Monetary Fund, International Financial Statistics, various issues.

Note: Figures for 1867-1959 are as given by the Wholesale Price Index excluding gold. Data for 1960-1974 were consolidated to 1958 = 100 and then converted to 1935-39 = 100.

CANADA
LONG-TERM GOVERNMENT BOND YIELD
1900 TO 1974

Year	Yield	Year	Yield	Year	Yield	Year	Yield
1900	3.34	1920	5.77	1940	3.28	1960	5.26
01	3.50	21	5.88	41	3.10	61	5.08
02	3.52	22	5.34	42	3.06	62	5.09
03	3.49	23	5.05	43	3.01	63	5.07
04	3.51	24	4.90	44	2.99	64	5.19
05	3.36	25	4.81	45	2.93	65	5.22
06	3.40	26	4.84	46	2.61	66	5.74
07	3.77	27	4.65	47	2.56	67	5.96
08	3.87	28	4.48	48	2.93	68	6.75
09	3.54	29	4.93	49	2.82	69	7.58
1910	3.68	1930	4.73	1950	2.78	1970	7.91
11	3.67	31	4.65	51	3.24	71	6.95
12	3.87	32	5.14	52	3.59	72	7.23
13	4.07	33	4.55	53	3.68	73	7.56
14	4.02	34	3.91	54	3.14	74	8.90
15	4.41	35	3.39	55	3.08		
16	4.85	36	2.97	56	3.61		
17	5.24	37	3.17	57	4.17		
18	5.74	38	3.09	58	4.26		
19	5.36	39	3.16	59	5.17		

Sources: 1900-1962 from Homer, S., 1963, A History of Interest Rates (Rutgers University Press, New Brunswick).
1963-1974 from International Monetary Fund, International Financial Statistics, various issues.

Note: Interest rate for 1900-1919 is the average annual yield on Province of Ontario bonds less 27 basis points. Interest rate for 1919-1974 is the average annual yield on Canadian dollar bonds.

FRANCE
WHOLESALE PRICE INDEX, 1798 TO 1974
1901-1910 = 100

1798	181	1838	131	1878	120	1918	389
99	179	39	130	79	117	19	403
1800	181	1840	135	1880	120	1920	576
01	161	41	134	81	117	21	396
02	159	42	131	82	114	22	375
03	170	43	121	83	110	23	479
04	159	44	118	84	101	24	555
05	174	45	121	85	99	25	625
06	191	46	129	86	95	26	798
07	187	47	136	87	92	27	701
08	246	48	112	88	96	28	708
09	246	49	111	89	100	29	694
1810	254	1850	111	1890	100	1930	604
11	251	51	110	91	98	31	514
12	262	52	119	92	95	32	451
13	245	53	139	93	94	33	430
14	187	54	148	94	87	34	410
15	177	55	154	95	85	35	389
16	184	56	156	96	82	36	451
17	197	57	151	97	83	37	625
18	188	58	137	98	86	38	715
19	161	59	137	99	93	39	750
1820	153	1860	144	1900	99	1940	986
21	143	61	142	01	95	41	1,208
22	138	62	142	02	94	42	1,409
23	143	63	143	03	96	43	1,638
24	133	64	141	04	94	44	1,846
25	146	65	132	05	98	45	2,610
26	136	66	134	06	104	46	4,498
27	134	67	131	07	109	47	6,844
28	129	68	132	08	101	48	11,793
29	130	69	130	09	101	49	13,063
1830	130	1870	133	1910	108	1950	14,152
31	124	71	138	11	113	51	18,143
32	125	72	144	12	118	52	19,050
33	126	73	144	13	116	53	18,143
34	128	74	132	14	118	54	17,780
35	132	75	129	15	160	55	17,780
36	135	76	130	16	215	56	18,506
37	126	77	131	17	298	57	19,594

FRANCE
WHOLESALE PRICE INDEX (continued)

1958	21,953	1962	24,674	1967	26,852	1971	32,257
59	22,860	63	25,582	68	27,033	72	33,742
		64	25,944	69	29,392	73	38,703
1960	23,586	65	26,307			74	49,982
61	23,949	66	26,852	1970	31,594		

Sources: 1798-1969 from Mitchell, B. R., 1975, European Historical Statistics 1750-1970 (The Macmillan Press LTD, London).
    1970-1974 from United Nations, Monthly Bulletin of Statistics, Vol. 29, No. 9.

Note: Data for 1798 to 1969 were converted to 1901-1910 = 100 using (single) overlap years given. Figures for 1970-74 are as given by the Index of Wholesale Prices--Industrial Products and were converted from 1970 = 100 to 1901-1910 = 100 using the average ratio of Mitchell's series (converted to 1901-1910 = 100) to the United Nations' series for the years 1966-1969.

FRANCE
LONG-TERM GOVERNMENT BOND YIELD
1798 TO 1974

1798	29.41	1838	3.74	1878	4.06	1918	4.94
99	33.31	39	3.74	79	3.73	19	4.82
1800	15.89	1840	3.98	1880	3.56	1920	5.30
01	8.61	41	3.84	81	3.54	21	5.30
02	8.31	42	3.78	82	3.67	22	5.05
03	8.11	43	3.71	83	3.83	23	5.42
04	8.21	44	3.63	84	3.88	24	5.58
05	8.01	45	3.58	85	3.79	25	6.37
06	6.61	46	3.63	86	3.66	26	6.15
07	5.41	47	3.88	87	3.78	27	4.60
08	5.29	48	5.58	88	3.63	28	4.35
09	5.56	49	5.80	89	3.51	29	4.08
1810	5.46	1850	5.33	1890	3.26	1930	3.44
11	5.53	51	4.94	91	3.18	31	3.48
12	5.56	52	4.00	92	3.07	32	3.84
13	7.21	53	3.90	93	3.10	33	4.38
14	7.31	54	4.34	94	2.98	34	4.14
15	6.76	55	4.42	95	2.96	35	3.88
16	7.66	56	4.39	96	2.94	36	4.32
17	7.46	57	4.39	97	2.90	37	4.27
18	6.51	58	4.21	98	2.92	38	4.04
19	6.56	59	4.55	99	2.98	39	3.97
1820	6.01	1860	4.34	1900	2.98	1940	4.06
21	5.46	61	4.38	01	2.96	41	3.19
22	4.91	62	4.28	02	2.99	42	3.14
23	5.26	63	4.39	03	3.06	43	3.11
24	4.35	64	4.54	04	3.11	44	3.01
25	4.40	65	4.42	05	3.03	45	2.99
26	4.42	66	4.55	06	3.08	46	3.17
27	4.30	67	4.41	07	3.16	47	3.91
28	4.20	68	4.27	08	3.13	48	4.62
29	3.75	69	4.17	09	3.07	49	4.78
1830	4.28	1870	4.76	1910	3.06	1950	5.02
31	5.15	71	5.51	11	3.14	51	5.31
32	4.51	72	5.47	12	3.27	52	4.81
33	3.98	73	5.34	13	3.44	53	4.93
34	3.91	74	4.90	14	3.78	54	4.53
35	3.77	75	4.66	15	4.36	55	4.25
36	3.77	76	4.35	16	4.80	56	4.59
37	3.76	77	4.27	17	4.95	57	5.16

FRANCE
LONG-TERM GOVERNMENT BOND YIELD (continued)

1958	3.92	1962	3.76	1967	4.40	1971	5.98
59	3.41	63	3.71	68	4.60	72	5.59
		64	3.82	69	5.17	73	6.49
1960	3.54	65	4.01			74	8.73
61	3.81	66	4.14	1970	6.30		

Sources: 1798-1961 from Homer, S., 1963, *A History of Interest Rates* (Rutgers University Press, New Brunswick).
1962-1974 from International Monetary Fund, *International Financial Statistics*, various issues.

Note: Interest rate for 1798-1824 is the average annual yield on 5% Rentes less 69 basis points. Interest rate for 1825-1961 is the average annual yield on 3% Rentes. Interest rate for 1962-1970 is the yield on the 5% perpetuities of 1949 less 126 basis points. Interest rate for 1971-1974 is the average of yields to maturity of the National Equipment Bonds of 1965, 1966, and 1967 less 176 basis points.

GERMANY
WHOLESALE PRICE INDEX, 1792 TO 1921
1913 = 100

Year	Index	Year	Index	Year	Index	Year	Index
1792	98	1825	76	1858	91	1890	86.5
93	98	26	72	59	89	91	86
94	101	27	77			92	80
95	122	28	78	1860	94	93	77
96	114	29	77	61	94	94	73
97	108			62	94	95	72
98	116	1830	78	63	92	96	72
99	132	31	82	64	91	97	76
		32	80	65	89	98	79
1800	135	33	76	66	90	99	83
01	134	34	76	67	97		
02	131	35	77	68	97	1900	90
03	139	36	78	69	92	01	83
04	136	37	74			02	81
05	156	38	78	1870	92	03	82
06	157	39	81	71	100	04	82
07	148			72	114	05	86
08	176	1840	80	73	120	06	92
09	156	41	78	74	112	07	97
		42	78	75	100	08	90
1810	132	43	77.5	76	95	09	91
11	123	44	76	77	91		
12	137	45	82	78	83	1910	93
13	120	46	88	79	81	11	94
14	110	47	97			12	102
15	112	48	76	1880	87	13	100
16	124	49	70	81	85	14	105
17	148			82	81	15	140
18	130	1850	71	83	80	16	150
19	103	51	75	84	78	17	177
		52	82	85	75	18	216
1820	90	53	92	86	72	19	413
21	85	54	100	87	73		
22	84	55	105	88	75	1920	1476
23	82	56	105	89	82	21	1899
24	72	57	101				

Source: Mitchell, B. R., 1975, <u>European Historical Statistics 1750-1970</u> (The Macmillan Press, London).

Note: Data were consolidated to 1913 = 100 using overlap year of 1914.

GERMANY
LONG-TERM INTEREST RATE
1815 TO 1921

Year	Rate	Year	Rate	Year	Rate	Year	Rate
1815	4.43	1842	3.32	1870	4.60	1898	3.40
16	4.68	43	3.33	71	4.44	99	3.55
17	4.95	44	3.32	72	4.26		
18	5.35	45	3.39	73	4.30	1900	3.68
19	5.28	46	3.56	74	4.24	01	3.65
		47	3.66	75	4.25	02	3.52
1820	5.21	48	4.47	76	4.21	03	3.53
21	5.36	49	4.00	77	4.22	04	3.57
22	4.96			78	4.26	05	3.57
23	4.96	1850	3.97	79	4.17	06	3.63
24	3.89	51	3.86			07	3.75
25	3.90	52	3.63	1880	4.05	08	3.80
26	4.23	53	3.69	81	3.96	09	3.70
27	4.03	54	4.08	82	3.94		
28	3.90	55	3.97	83	3.92	1910	3.76
29	3.61	56	4.02	84	3.88	11	3.79
		57	4.10	85	3.81	12	3.91
1830	3.58	58	4.02	86	3.74	13	4.09
31	3.90	59	4.16	87	3.70	14	5.06
32	3.76			88	3.64	15	5.06
33	3.62	1860	3.98	89	3.60	16	5.10
34	3.52	61	3.89			17	5.11
35	3.45	62	3.90	1890	3.68	18	5.11
36	3.43	63	3.90	91	3.71	19	6.20
37	3.40	64	4.00	92	3.68		
38	3.39	65	3.99	93	3.65	1920	6.34
39	3.35	66	4.43	94	3.56	21	6.45
		67	4.38	95	3.36		
1840	3.35	68	4.38	96	3.35		
41	3.33	69	4.48	97	3.36		

Source: Homer, S., 1963, *A History of Interest Rates* (Rutgers University Press, New Brunswick).

Note: Interest rate for 1815-1843 is the average annual yield on Prussian State 4% bonds less 51 basis points. Interest rate for 1844-1859 is the average annual yield on Prussian State 3-1/2% bonds less 13 basis points. Interest rate for 1860-1869 is the average annual yield on Bavarian 4% bonds less 6 basis points. Interest rate for 1870-1921 is an average of high-grade bond yields.

GREAT BRITAIN
WHOLESALE PRICE INDEX, 1729 TO 1974
1867-1877 = 100

Year	Index	Year	Index	Year	Index	Year	Index
1729	79.6	1769	76.4	1809	160.4	1849	74
1730	77.2	1770	77.6	1810	158.8	1850	77
31	73.2	71	80.4	11	150.5	51	75
32	71.6	72	86.0	12	169.4	52	78
33	68.4	73	87.2	13	174.8	53	95
34	69.6	74	85.6	14	159.1	54	102
35	68.8	75	84.4	15	134.4	55	101
36	67.6	76	86.0	16	122.8	56	101
37	69.6	77	84.0	17	136.5	57	105
38	68.8	78	88.4	18	143.6	58	91
39	70.4	79	88.4	19	132.6	59	94
1740	75.6	1780	89.2	1820	119.4	1860	99
41	82.0	81	90.0	21	103.2	61	98
42	78.4	82	94.4	22	91.0	62	101
43	74.0	83	98.4	23	101.0	63	103
44	72.8	84	93.6	24	105.5	64	105
45	66.4	85	90.8	25	117.0	65	101
46	73.6	86	92.8	26	103.5	66	102
47	70.4	87	91.2	27	102.8	67	100
48	73.2	88	93.6	28	99.8	68	99
49	74.8	89	89.6	29	99.2	69	98
1750	73.2	1790	92.4	1830	97.8	1870	96
51	70.0	91	92.8	31	98.6	71	100
52	69.6	92	91.2	32	94.7	72	109
53	68.4	93	100.0	33	91.7	73	111
54	71.6	94	101.9	34	89.5	74	102
55	73.2	95	118.9	35	87.5	75	96
56	74.0	96	120.2	36	98.5	76	95
57	81.2	97	109.9	37	97.6	77	94
58	82.8	98	111.7	38	101.2	78	87
59	80.4	99	129.0	39	108.0	79	83
1760	80.0	1800	156.3	1840	106.1	1880	88
61	78.0	01	161.1	41	101.1	81	85
62	78.4	02	126.5	42	91.9	82	84
63	80.8	03	127.9	43	82.5	83	82
64	81.2	04	128.7	44	83.9	84	76
65	82.0	05	141.0	45	86.2	85	72
66	82.4	06	139.2	46	89	86	69
67	83.2	07	135.8	47	95	87	68
68	82.4	08	149.6	48	78	88	70

GREAT BRITAIN
WHOLESALE PRICE INDEX (continued)

Year	Value	Year	Value	Year	Value	Year	Value
1889	72	1911	80	1934	82	1957	376
		12	85	35	84	58	355
1890	72	13	85	36	89	59	356
91	72	14	85	37	102		
92	68	15	108	38	90	1960	359
93	68	16	136	39	94	61	354
94	63	17	179			62	360
95	62	18	192	1940	128	63	374
96	61	19	206	41	142	64	401
97	62			42	151	65	404
98	64	1920	251	43	155	66	417
99	68	21	155	44	160	67	423
		22	131	45	164	68	444
1900	75	23	129	46	186	69	461
01	70	24	139	47	230		
02	69	25	136	48	260	1970	494
03	69	26	126	49	274	71	539
04	70	27	122			72	567
05	72	28	120	1950	324	73	609
06	77	29	115	51	401	74	752
07	80			52	380		
08	73	1930	97	53	366		
09	74	31	83	54	361		
		32	80	55	370		
1910	78	33	79	56	384		

Sources: 1729-1937 from Mitchell, B. R., 1962, <u>Abstract of British Historical Statistics</u> (Cambridge University Press, Cambridge).
    1938-1965 from Mitchell, B. R., and Jones, H. G., 1971, <u>Second Abstract of British Historical Statistics</u> (Cambridge University Press, Cambridge).
    1965-1972 from Great Britain Central Statistical Office, <u>Annual Abstract of Statistics</u>, various issues.
    1973-1974 from International Monetary Fund, <u>International Financial Statistics</u>. (Series used is Prices: Industrial Output.)

Note: Figures for 1729-1789 are as given by the Schumpter-Gilboy Price index (unweighted average of consumers' and producers' goods) converted from 1697=100 to 1867-1877=100 using overlap year of 1790. Figures for 1790-1845 are as given by the Gayer, Rostow, and Schwartz index of British commodity prices (domestic and imported commodities) converted from 1821-1825=100 to 1867-1877=100 using overlap year of 1846. Figures for 1846-1965 are as given by the Sauerbeck-Statist Price Index, 1867-1877=100. Figures for 1966-1974 are as given by the Wholesale Price Index of the Output of Manufactured Products consolidated to 1963=100 and then converted to 1867-1877=100 using overlap year of 1965.

GREAT BRITAIN
LONG-TERM GOVERNMENT BOND YIELD
1729 TO 1974

Year	Yield	Year	Yield	Year	Yield	Year	Yield
1729	3.24	1769	3.47	1809	4.49	1849	3.24
1730	3.30	1770	3.64	1810	4.47	1850	3.11
31	3.12	71	3.55	11	4.67	51	3.09
32	3.03	72	3.30	12	5.08	52	3.02
33	3.09	73	3.47	13	4.92	53	3.07
34	3.19	74	3.43	14	4.92	54	3.27
35	3.19	75	3.39	15	4.48	55	3.31
36	2.86	76	3.51	16	5.02	56	3.22
37	2.83	77	3.85	17	4.10	57	3.27
38	2.86	78	4.51	18	3.87	58	3.10
39	3.06	79	4.88	19	4.17	59	3.15
1740	3.00	1780	4.88	1820	4.42	1860	3.19
41	3.03	81	5.22	21	4.07	61	3.28
42	3.00	82	5.26	22	3.79	62	3.23
43	2.97	83	4.76	23	3.80	63	3.24
44	3.24	84	5.41	24	3.30	64	3.33
45	3.53	85	4.76	25	3.54	65	3.35
46	3.41	86	4.06	26	3.79	66	3.41
47	3.66	87	4.08	27	3.61	67	3.23
48	3.41	88	4.06	28	3.54	68	3.20
49	2.97	89	3.92	29	3.34	69	3.23
1750	3.00	1790	3.90	1830	3.49	1870	3.24
51	3.03	91	3.58	31	3.76	71	3.23
52	2.86	92	3.33	32	3.58	72	3.24
53	2.86	93	3.96	33	3.42	73	3.24
54	2.91	94	4.40	34	3.32	74	3.24
55	3.14	95	4.52	35	3.29	75	3.20
56	3.37	96	4.80	36	3.35	76	3.16
57	3.39	97	5.90	37	3.30	77	3.15
58	3.21	98	5.94	38	3.23	78	3.15
59	3.59	99	5.07	39	3.28	79	3.08
1760	3.77	1800	4.71	1840	3.35	1880	3.05
61	3.90	01	4.92	41	3.38	81	3.00
62	4.29	02	4.23	42	3.27	82	2.99
63	3.37	03	4.99	43	3.17	83	2.97
64	3.61	04	5.30	44	3.03	84	2.97
65	3.41	05	5.04	45	3.12	85	3.02
66	3.39	06	4.87	46	3.13	86	2.98
67	3.37	07	4.92	47	3.44	87	2.95
68	3.31	08	4.55	48	3.51	88	2.97

GREAT BRITAIN
LONG-TERM GOVERNMENT BOND YIELD (continued)

Year	Yield	Year	Yield	Year	Yield	Year	Yield
1889	2.81	1911	3.15	1934	3.08	1957	4.98
		12	3.28	35	2.89	58	4.98
1890	2.67	13	3.39	36	2.94	59	4.82
91	2.70	14	3.46	37	3.28		
92	2.65	15	3.82	38	3.38	1960	5.40
93	2.61	16	4.31	39	3.72	61	6.20
94	2.52	17	4.58			62	5.98
95	2.39	18	4.40	1940	3.40	63	5.58
96	2.28	19	4.62	41	3.13	64	6.03
97	2.25			42	3.03	65	6.42
98	2.28	1920	5.32	43	3.10	66	6.80
99	2.36	21	5.21	44	3.14	67	6.69
		22	4.43	45	2.92	68	7.39
1900	2.54	23	4.31	46	2.60	69	8.88
01	2.67	24	4.39	47	2.76		
02	2.66	25	4.43	48	3.21	1970	9.16
03	2.75	26	4.55	49	3.30	71	9.05
04	2.83	27	4.56			72	9.11
05	2.78	28	4.47	1950	3.35	73	10.85
06	2.83	29	4.60	51	3.79	74	14.95
07	2.97			52	4.23		
08	2.90	1930	4.46	53	4.08		
09	2.98	31	4.53	54	3.76		
		32	3.76	55	4.17		
1910	3.08	33	3.38	56	4.74		

Sources: 1729-1961 from Homer, S., 1963, <u>A History of Interest Rates</u> (Rutgers University Press, New Brunswick).
    1962-1972 from Great Britain Central Statistical Office, <u>Annual Abstract of Statistics</u>, various issues.
    1973-1974 from Great Britain Central Statistical Office, <u>Monthly Digest of Statistics</u>, December, 1975.

Note: Interest rate for 1729-1752 is the average annual yield on the Old 3% Annuities. Interest rate for 1753-1888 is the average annual yield on 3% Consols. Interest rate for 1889-1903 is the average annual yield on 2-1/2% consols paying an extra 1/4%. Interest rate for 1904-1974 is the average annual yield on 2-1/2% consols.

ITALY
WHOLESALE PRICE INDEX, 1861 TO 1974
1929 = 100

Year	Index	Year	Index	Year	Index	Year	Index
1861	20.4	1890	18.3	1919	93	1947	5,154
62	19.0	91	17.7			48	5,437
63	18.1	92	16.9	1920	122	49	5,123
64	18.1	93	15.8	21	112		
65	17.9	94	15.4	22	112	1950	4,862
66	18.7	95	16.2	23	113	51	5,541
67	18.7	96	16.2	24	113	52	5,228
68	20.0	97	16.0	25	126	53	5,228
69	18.5	98	16.5	26	129	54	5,176
		99	16.9	27	108	55	5,228
1870	18.4			28	105	56	5,332
71	19.1	1900	17.6	29	100	57	5,385
72	20.6	01	17.5			58	5,280
73	21.9	02	16.9	1930	90	59	5,123
74	21.9	03	16.9	31	78		
75	19.4	04	16.0	32	73	1960	5,176
76	18.7	05	16.7	33	66	61	5,176
77	21.2	06	17.3	34	65	62	5,332
78	20.6	07	18.7	35	71	63	5,594
79	19.4	08	18.1	36	80	64	5,803
		09	18.3	37	93	65	5,907
1880	19.4			38	100	66	5,960
81	18.1	1910	18.3	39	104	67	5,907
82	18.7	11	19.8			68	5,960
83	17.5	12	21.5	1940	122	69	6,221
84	16.7	13	20.8	41	136		
85	17.7	14	20	42	152	1970	6,675
86	17.7	15	26	43	229	71	6,902
87	16.5	16	38	44	857	72	7,182
88	16.9	17	57	45	2,058	73	8,404
89	17.7	18	85	46	2,881	74	11,828

Sources: 1861-1969 from Mitchell, B. R., 1975, European Historical Statistics 1750-1970 (The Macmillan Press LTD, London).
 1970-1974 from International Monetary Fund, International Financial Statistics, Vol. 29, No. 5.

Note: Data for 1861-1969 were consolidated to 1929 = 100. Data for 1970-1974 were converted to 1929 = 100 using overlap year of 1969.

ITALY
LONG-TERM GOVERNMENT BOND YIELD
1924-1974

Year	Yield	Year	Yield	Year	Yield	Year	Yield
1924	5.67	1937	5.41	1950	5.39	1963	5.61
25	5.98	38	5.41	51	5.68	64	6.92
26	6.88	39	5.48	52	5.83	65	6.45
27	6.54			53	6.06	66	6.05
28	6.87	1940	5.45	54	6.06	67	6.12
29	5.74	41	5.27	55	6.20	68	6.21
		42	4.84	56	6.74	69	6.36
1930	5.81	43	4.66	57	6.81		
31	5.50	44	3.96	58	6.16	1970	8.52
32	5.37	45	3.82	59	5.43	71	7.85
33	4.95	46	4.41			72	6.98
34	4.69	47	5.03	1960	5.24	73	6.93
35	5.39	48	5.00	61	5.18	74	9.38
36	5.34	49	5.12	62	5.29		

Sources: 1924-1962 from Homer, S., 1963, *A History of Interest Rates* (Rutgers University Press, New Brunswick).
1963-1974 from International Monetary Fund, *International Financial Statistics*, Vol. 29, No. 5.

Note: Interest rate for 1924-1952 is the yield on the (irredeemable) 3-1/2% bonds of 1906 plus 60 basis points. Interest rate for 1953-1962 is the yield to maturity on the 5% bonds due 1978. Interest rate for 1963-1974 is the Long-Term Government Bond Yield less 49 basis points.

NETHERLANDS
WHOLESALE PRICE INDEX, 1901 TO 1974
1929 = 100

Year	Index	Year	Index	Year	Index	Year	Index
1901	65	1920	196	1939	73	1957	283
02	65	21	153			58	278
03	65	22	120	1940	92	59	281
04	67	23	112	41	104		
05	69	24	118	42	110	1960	275
06	69	25	118	43	112	61	273
07	71	26	106	44	114	62	275
08	71	27	102	45	125	63	281
09	73	28	102	46	175	64	299
		29	100	47	188	65	307
1910	71			48	196	66	323
11	78	1930	88	49	207	67	323
12	80	31	75			68	326
13	75	32	65	1950	230	69	328
14	80	33	63	51	283		
15	108	34	63	52	275	1970	349
16	165	35	61	53	265	71	352
17	186	36	63	54	268	72	364
18	210	37	75	55	270	73	410
19	212	38	71	56	275	74	467

Sources: 1901-1969 from Mitchell, B. R., 1975, European Historical Statistics 1750-1970 (The Macmillan Press LTD, London).
1970-1974 from United Nations, Monthly Bulletin of Statistics, Vol. 30, No. 4.

Note: Data for 1901-1969 were consolidated to 1929 = 100 using overlap year of 1948. Data for 1970-1974 were converted to 1929 = 100 using overlap year of 1969.

NETHERLANDS
LONG-TERM GOVERNMENT BOND YIELD
1814 TO 1974

Year	Yield	Year	Yield	Year	Yield	Year	Yield
1814	6.66	1855	3.98	1896	2.80	1937	3.13
15	6.09	56	3.94	97	2.84	38	2.99
16	5.69	57	3.94	98	2.88	39	3.56
17	5.76	58	3.88	99	3.14		
18	5.80	59	3.90			1940	3.98
19	5.70			1900	3.29	41	3.68
		1860	4.00	01	3.24	42	3.21
1820	5.52	61	3.97	02	3.07	43	3.11
21	5.25	62	3.89	03	3.11	44	3.09
22	5.25	63	3.92	04	3.12	45	3.01
23	5.20	64	4.01	05	3.16	46	2.99
24	4.29	65	4.05	06	3.17	47	3.06
25	4.45	66	4.50	07	3.31	48	3.09
26	4.90	67	4.76	08	3.31	49	3.12
27	4.76	68	4.39	09	3.27		
28	4.37	69	4.65			1950	3.12
29	3.94			1910	3.35	51	3.42
		1870	4.75	11	3.52	52	3.41
1830	6.22	71	4.33	12	3.71	53	3.18
31	6.02	72	4.66	13	3.50	54	3.16
32	5.97	73	4.33	14	3.49	55	3.18
33	5.00	74	4.01	15	3.95	56	3.42
34	4.62	75	3.96	16	4.09	57	4.05
35	4.54	76	3.96	17	4.12	58	4.07
36	4.62	77	3.91	18	4.52	59	4.17
37	4.75	78	3.98	19	5.00		
38	4.60	79	3.86			1960	4.27
39	4.79			1920	5.56	61	4.10
		1880	3.84	21	5.21	62	4.40
1840	5.01	81	3.72	22	4.86	63	4.41
41	4.85	82	3.75	23	4.63	64	5.11
42	4.78	83	3.84	24	4.70	65	5.21
43	4.56	84	3.75	25	4.18	66	6.30
44	3.84	85	3.60	26	4.00	67	5.89
45	4.04	86	3.36	27	4.01	68	6.20
46	4.18	87	3.38	28	3.88	69	7.22
47	4.52	88	3.25	29	3.94		
48	5.02	89	2.99			1970	7.93
49	4.51			1930	3.81	71	7.06
		1890	3.19	31	3.86	72	6.59
1850	4.36	91	3.15	32	3.89	73	7.50
51	4.28	92	3.01	33	3.68	74	9.41
52	3.76	93	2.96	34	3.35		
53	3.99	94	2.66	35	3.43		
54	4.16	95	2.69	36	3.32		

NETHERLANDS
LONG-TERM GOVERNMENT BOND YIELD (continued)

Sources: 1814 to 1961 from Homer, S. 1963, A History of Interest Rates (Rutgers University Press, New Brunswick).
1962-1974 from International Monetary Fund, International Financial Statistics, Vol. 20, No. 8 and Vol. 29, No. 5.

Note: Interest rate for 1814-1961 is the average annual yield on 2-1/2% Perpetual Debt of the Central Government. Interest rate for 1962-1965 is the yield to redemption (1984) on the 3-1/2% bond maturing in June, 1998 plus 19 basis points. Interest rate for 1966-1974 is the unweighted average yield on the 5% and 5-1/4% government bond issues maturing in 1982 less 29 basis points.

SWITZERLAND
WHOLESALE PRICE INDEX, 1921 TO 1974
1929 = 100

1921	139	1935	64	1949	157	1962	170
22	118	36	68			63	176
23	128	37	79	1950	155	64	180
24	125	38	76	51	173	65	181
25	116	39	79	52	168	66	184
26	103			53	162	67	184
27	101	1940	101	54	163	68	184
28	103	41	130	55	163	69	191
29	100	42	149	56	168		
		43	155	57	170	1970	199
1930	89	44	158	58	165	71	203
31	78	45	157	59	162	72	211
32	68	46	152			73	233
33	65	47	159	1960	163	74	271
34	64	48	165	61	163		

Sources: 1921-1969 from Mitchell, B. R., 1975, European Historical Statistics 1750-1970 (The Macmillan Press LTD, London).
    1970-1974 from United Nations, Monthly Bulletin of Statistics, Vol. 30, No. 4.

Note: Data for 1921-1969 were consolidated to 1929 = 100. Figures for 1970-1974 are as given by the General Index of Wholesale Prices converted to 1929 = 100 using overlap year of 1969.

SWITZERLAND
LONG-TERM GOVERNMENT BOND YIELD
1916 TO 1974

Year	Yield	Year	Yield	Year	Yield	Year	Yield
1916	4.85	1931	3.86	1947	3.17	1962	3.12
17	5.03	32	3.80	48	3.42	63	3.24
18	5.34	33	4.02	49	2.94	64	3.96
19	5.56	34	4.16			65	3.94
		35	4.64	1950	2.67	66	4.15
1920	7.00	36	4.43	51	2.95	67	4.60
21	6.10	37	3.41	52	2.84	68	4.36
22	4.80	38	3.24	53	2.55	69	4.89
23	4.79	39	3.76	54	2.62		
24	5.31			55	2.97	1970	5.81
25	5.05	1940	4.06	56	3.11	71	5.26
26	4.80	41	3.39	57	3.64	72	4.96
27	4.79	42	3.15	58	3.19	73	5.59
28	4.73	43	3.32	59	3.08	74	7.14
29	4.66	44	3.27				
		45	3.29	1960	3.09		
1930	4.12	46	3.10	61	2.96		

Sources: 1916-1962 from Homer, S., 1963, A History of Interest Rates (Rutgers University Press, New Brunswick).
1963-1974 from International Monetary Fund, International Financial Statistics, Vol. 29, No. 5.

Note: Interest rate for 1916-1962 is the weighted average of yields to maturity of twelve Government and Federal Railway bond issues with maturity of at least five years. Interest rate for 1963-1974 is the Government Bond Yield less 1 basis point.

UNITED STATES
WHOLESALE PRICE INDEX, 1870 TO 1974
1967 = 100

Year	Index	Year	Index	Year	Index	Year	Index
1870	47.5	1900	28.9	1930	44.6	1960	94.9
71	45.4	01	28.5	31	37.6	61	94.5
72	48.4	02	30.4	32	33.6	62	94.8
73	46.5	03	30.7	33	34.0	63	94.5
74	44.0	04	30.8	34	38.6	64	94.7
75	41.7	05	31.0	35	41.3	65	96.6
76	38.4	06	32.0	36	41.7	66	99.8
77	37.3	07	33.6	37	44.5	67	100.0
78	31.9	08	32.4	38	40.5	68	102.5
79	31.3	09	34.9	39	39.8	69	106.5
1880	35.0	1910	36.4	1940	40.5	1970	110.4
81	35.5	11	33.5	41	45.1	71	113.9
82	37.0	12	35.6	42	50.9	72	119.1
83	34.3	13	36.0	43	53.3	73	134.7
84	31.9	14	35.2	44	53.6	74	160.1
85	29.4	15	35.8	45	54.6		
86	28.3	16	44.1	46	62.3		
87	29.4	17	60.6	47	76.5		
88	30.0	18	67.6	48	82.8		
89	28.7	19	71.4	49	78.7		
1890	28.9	1920	79.6	1950	81.8		
91	28.8	21	50.3	51	91.1		
92	26.9	22	49.9	52	88.6		
93	27.5	23	51.9	53	87.4		
94	24.7	24	50.5	54	87.6		
95	25.2	25	53.3	55	87.8		
96	23.9	26	51.6	56	90.7		
97	24.0	27	49.3	57	93.3		
98	25.0	28	50.0	58	94.6		
99	26.9	29	49.1	59	94.8		

Sources: 1870-1970 from United States Department of Commerce, Long-Term Economic Growth, 1860-1970.
    1971-1974 from United States Department of Commerce, Business Statistics, 1975 ed..

UNITED STATES
LONG-TERM INTEREST RATE
1870 TO 1974

Year	Rate	Year	Rate	Year	Rate	Year	Rate
1870	6.53	1900	3.30	1930	4.40	1960	4.55
71	6.46	01	3.25	31	4.10	61	4.22
72	6.31	02	3.30	32	4.70	62	4.42
73	6.33	03	3.45	33	4.15	63	4.16
74	6.02	04	3.60	34	3.99	64	4.33
75	5.58	05	3.50	35	3.50	65	4.35
76	5.29	06	3.55	36	3.20	66	4.75
77	5.30	07	3.80	37	3.08	67	4.95
78	5.22	08	3.95	38	3.00	68	5.93
79	4.88	09	3.77	39	2.75	69	6.54
1880	4.59	1910	3.80	1940	2.70	1970	7.60
81	4.26	11	3.90	41	2.65	71	6.95
82	4.32	12	3.90	42	2.65	72	6.77
83	4.34	13	4.00	43	2.65	73	7.00
84	4.29	14	4.10	44	2.60	74	8.13
85	4.09	15	4.15	45	2.55		
86	3.82	16	4.05	46	2.43		
87	3.88	17	4.05	47	2.50		
88	3.81	18	4.75	48	2.80		
89	3.66	19	4.75	49	2.74		
1890	3.79	1920	5.10	1950	2.58		
91	3.95	21	5.17	51	2.67		
92	3.84	22	4.71	52	3.00		
93	3.94	23	4.61	53	3.15		
94	3.72	24	4.66	54	3.00		
95	3.59	25	4.50	55	3.04		
96	3.64	26	4.40	56	3.09		
97	3.44	27	4.30	57	3.68		
98	3.38	28	4.05	58	3.61		
99	3.25	29	4.42	59	4.10		

Sources: 1870-1970 from United States Department of Commerce, Long-Term Economic Growth, 1860-1970.
1971-1974 from United States Department of Commerce, Business Statistics, 1975 ed..

Note: Interest rate for 1870-1899 is Macaulay's Adjusted Index of American Railroad Bond yields plus 12 basis points. Interest rate for 1900-1970 is the NBER-Durand-Homer basic yield on 30-year corporate bonds. Interest rate for 1971-1974 is the yield on Moody's Aaa Domestic Corporate Bonds less 44 basis points.

UNITED STATES
GROSS NATIONAL PRODUCT, 1890 TO 1969
BILLIONS OF 1958 DOLLARS

1890	54.7	1910	120.1	1930	183.5	1950	355.3
91	57.2	11	123.2	31	169.3	51	383.4
92	62.7	12	130.2	32	144.2	52	395.1
93	59.7	13	131.4	33	141.5	53	412.8
94	58.0	14	125.6	34	154.3	54	407.0
95	64.9	15	124.5	35	169.5	55	438.0
96	63.6	16	134.3	36	193.0	56	446.1
97	69.6	17	135.2	37	203.2	57	452.5
98	71.1	18	151.8	38	192.9	58	447.3
99	77.7	19	146.4	39	209.4	59	475.9
1900	79.7	1920	140.0	1940	227.2	1960	487.7
01	89.0	21	127.8	41	263.7	61	497.2
02	89.8	22	148.0	42	297.8	62	529.8
03	94.3	23	165.9	43	337.1	63	551.0
04	93.1	24	165.5	44	361.3	64	581.1
05	100.0	25	179.4	45	355.2	65	617.8
06	111.6	26	190.0	46	312.6	66	658.1
07	113.4	27	189.8	47	309.9	67	675.2
08	104.0	28	190.9	48	323.7	68	706.6
09	116.8	29	203.6	49	324.1	69	725.6

Sources: 1890-1968 from United States Department of Commerce, Long-Term Economic Growth, 1860-1970.
1969 from United States Department of Commerce, Survey of Current Business.

Note: Data for 1890-1908 are the NBER-Kendrick estimates. Data for 1909-1969 are the Bureau of Economic Analysis estimates. These series were spliced together by multiplying the NBER-Kendrick estimates by the ratio of the BEA to the NBER-Kendrick estimates for the overlap year of 1909.

UNITED STATES
IMPLICIT PRICE DEFLATOR FOR GNP, 1890 TO 1969
1958 = 100

Year	Value	Year	Value	Year	Value	Year	Value
1890	25.4	1910	29.9	1930	49.3	1950	80.2
91	24.9	11	29.7	31	44.8	51	85.6
92	24.0	12	30.9	32	40.2	52	87.5
93	24.5	13	31.1	33	39.3	53	88.3
94	23.0	14	31.4	34	42.2	54	89.6
95	22.7	15	32.5	35	42.6	55	90.9
96	22.1	16	36.5	36	42.7	56	94.0
97	22.2	17	45.0	37	44.5	57	97.5
98	22.9	18	52.6	38	43.9	58	100.0
99	23.6	19	53.8	39	43.2	59	101.6
1900	24.7	1920	61.3	1940	43.9	1960	103.3
01	24.5	21	52.2	41	47.2	61	104.6
02	25.4	22	49.5	42	53.0	62	105.8
03	25.7	23	50.7	43	56.8	63	107.2
04	26.0	24	50.1	44	58.2	64	108.8
05	26.5	25	51.0	45	59.7	65	110.9
06	27.2	26	51.2	46	66.7	66	113.9
07	28.3	27	50.0	47	74.6	67	117.6
08	28.1	28	50.4	48	79.6	68	122.3
09	29.1	29	50.6	49	79.1	69	128.2

Source: United States Department of Commerce, Long-Term Economic Growth, 1860-1970.

Note: Data for 1890-1928 are Kendrick's estimates. Data for 1929-1969 are Bureau of Economic Analysis estimates. These series were spliced together by multiplying Kendrick's estimates by the ratio of BEA to Kendrick estimates for the overlap year of 1929.

UNITED STATES
MONEY STOCK, 1890 TO 1969
BILLIONS OF CURRENT DOLLARS

1890	3.92	1910	13.36	1930	45.66	1950	150.8
91	4.09	01	14.22	31	42.43	51	156.4
92	4.43	02	15.17	32	35.93	52	164.9
93	4.26	03	15.76	33	32.09	53	171.1
94	4.28	04	16.42	34	34.53	54	177.2
95	4.43	05	17.70	35	39.28	55	183.7
96	4.35	06	21.00	36	43.67	56	186.8
97	4.64	07	23.91	37	45.64	57	191.8
98	5.26	08	25.94	38	45.62	58	201.2
99	6.09	09	31.20	39	49.47	59	210.4
1900	6.61	1920	34.85	1940	55.48	1960	212.5
01	7.48	21	32.74	41	62.77	61	225.0
02	8.17	22	33.88	42	71.78	62	240.8
03	8.68	23	36.66	43	90.75	63	259.6
04	9.25	24	38.71	44	107.47	64	279.6
05	10.24	25	42.18	45	127.37	65	304.7
06	11.08	26	43.68	46	139.10	66	328.7
07	11.60	27	44.81	47	146.0	67	355.1
08	11.49	28	46.49	48	148.1	68	386.9
09	12.73	29	46.57	49	147.5	69	405.4

Sources: 1890-1946 from Friedman, M., and Schwartz, A. J., 1970, Monetary Statistics of the United States: Estimates, Sources, Methods (Columbia University Press for the National Bureau of Economic Research).
1947-1969 from United States Department of Commerce, Business Statistics, 1973 ed..

Note: The money stock is the sum of currency held by the public and demand and time deposits held in commercial banks.

UNITED STATES
FEDERAL, STATE, AND LOCAL GOVERNMENT PURCHASES OF GOODS AND SERVICES
1890 TO 1969
BILLIONS OF CURRENT DOLLARS

1890	.661	1910	2.041	1930	9.2	1950	37.9
91	.694	11	2.464	31	9.2	51	59.1
92	.722	12	2.529	32	8.1	52	74.7
93	.756	13	2.482	33	8.0	53	81.6
94	.753	14	2.678	34	9.8	54	74.8
95	.773	15	2.808	35	10.0	55	74.2
96	.799	16	2.916	36	12.0	56	78.6
97	.844	17	5.361	37	11.9	57	86.1
98	1.034	18	16.196	38	13.0	58	94.2
99	1.098	19	9.456	39	13.3	59	97.0
1900	1.124	1920	5.904	1940	14.0	1960	99.6
01	1.148	21	6.301	41	24.8	61	107.6
02	1.237	22	5.952	42	59.6	62	117.1
03	1.413	23	6.186	43	88.6	63	122.5
04	1.366	24	6.701	44	96.5	64	128.7
05	1.527	25	7.256	45	82.3	65	137.0
06	1.620	26	7.297	46	27.0	66	156.8
07	1.891	27	7.864	47	25.1	67	180.1
08	2.108	28	8.184	48	31.6	68	199.6
09	1.924	29	8.482	49	37.8	69	210.0

Sources: 1890-1929 from Kendrick, J. W., 1961, Productivity Trends in the United States (Princeton University Press for the National Bureau of Economic Research).

1930-1969 from United States Department of Commerce, Historical Statistics of the United States: Colonial Times to 1970, September, 1970.

UNITED STATES
INDEX OF THE CIVILIAN LABOR FORCE, 1890 TO 1969
1958 = 100

Year	Index	Year	Index	Year	Index	Year	Index
1890	33.7	1910	54.3	1930	71.7	1950	92.0
91	34.5	11	55.4	31	72.9	51	91.7
92	35.3	12	56.1	32	74.1	52	91.9
93	36.2	13	57.2	33	75.2	53	93.2
94	37.0	14	58.3	34	76.4	54	94.1
95	37.9	15	58.5	35	77.3	55	96.1
96	38.7	16	59.2	36	78.4	56	98.4
97	39.5	17	59.2	37	79.5	57	99.0
98	40.1	18	57.8	38	80.6	58	100.0
99	41.1	19	58.7	39	81.6	59	101.1
1900	42.0	1920	61.1	1940	82.3	1960	102.9
01	43.1	21	62.1	41	82.7	61	104.2
02	44.2	22	62.8	42	83.4	62	104.4
03	45.4	23	64.2	43	82.1	63	106.2
04	46.5	24	65.4	44	80.8	64	108.1
05	47.8	25	66.8	45	79.6	65	110.1
06	49.1	26	67.5	46	85.0	66	112.0
07	50.5	27	68.6	47	87.7	67	114.4
08	51.6	28	69.6	48	89.6	68	116.4
09	52.8	29	70.6	49	90.6	69	119.4

Source: United States Department of Commerce, Long-Term Economic Growth, 1860-1970.

UNITED STATES
CAPITAL INPUT INDEX, 1890 TO 1969
1958 = 100

Year	Value	Year	Value	Year	Value	Year	Value
1890	19.1	1910	39.0	1930	62.6	1950	73.8
91	20.1	11	40.3	31	62.4	51	77.9
92	21.3	12	41.3	32	59.8	52	81.9
93	22.4	13	42.5	33	57.4	53	84.9
94	23.1	14	43.8	34	56.8	54	87.6
95	24.0	15	44.9	35	55.0	55	90.5
96	24.9	16	45.6	36	55.2	56	94.6
97	25.6	17	46.8	37	56.4	57	98.0
98	26.4	18	48.1	38	56.7	58	100.0
99	27.2	19	49.2	39	56.5	59	102.3
1900	28.3	1920	50.3	1940	57.2	1960	105.3
01	29.2	21	51.0	41	59.6	61	107.7
02	30.2	22	51.4	42	61.5	62	110.2
03	31.4	23	52.4	43	61.4	63	113.3
04	32.4	24	53.8	44	60.7	64	117.1
05	33.2	25	55.0	45	60.4	65	121.9
06	34.5	26	56.8	46	62.6	66	128.7
07	35.9	27	58.5	47	66.2	67	134.6
08	37.0	28	59.9	48	68.7	68	140.1
09	37.9	29	61.3	49	71.4	69	146.0

Source: United States Department of Commerce, <u>Long-Term Economic Growth, 1860-1970</u>.

UNITED STATES
INDEX OF FULL-EMPLOYMENT OUTPUT, 1890 TO 1969
1958 = 100

Year	Index	Year	Index	Year	Index	Year	Index
1890	27.6	1910	48.4	1930	68.4	1950	85.2
91	28.6	11	49.6	31	69.0	51	86.6
92	29.6	12	50.4	32	68.7	52	88.3
93	30.6	13	51.6	33	68.4	53	90.2
94	31.4	14	52.7	34	68.9	54	91.8
95	32.3	15	53.3	35	68.6	55	94.1
96	33.2	16	54.0	36	69.3	56	97.1
97	33.9	17	54.5	37	70.5	57	98.6
98	34.6	18	54.2	38	71.3	58	100.0
99	35.6	19	55.2	39	71.7	59	101.5
1900	36.6	1920	57.1	1940	72.5	1960	103.7
01	37.6	21	58.0	41	73.7	61	105.4
02	38.7	22	58.5	42	75.0	62	106.4
03	39.9	23	59.8	43	74.2	63	108.6
04	41.0	24	61.1	44	73.1	64	111.2
05	42.1	25	62.4	45	72.3	65	114.1
06	43.4	26	63.5	46	76.4	66	117.6
07	44.8	27	64.9	47	79.5	67	121.1
08	45.9	28	66.0	48	81.6	68	124.2
09	47.0	29	67.2	49	83.4	69	128.1

Note: This index (denoted k) is $k = K^{.35} \cdot L^{.65}$, K is the NBER-Kendrick Capital Input Index for the U.S. taken from United States Department of Commerce, Long-Term Economic Growth, 1860-1970, and L is the civilian labor force converted to an index with 1958 = 100, also taken from Long-Term Economic Growth, 1860-1970. The exponents .35 and .65 approximate the shares of capital and labor in total output. For a more complete discussion of this index, see page 65 in the text.

REFERENCES

Anderson, O. D., 1976, *Time Series Analysis and Forecasting: The Box-Jenkins Approach* (Butterworth & Co., London).

Barro, R. J., and Fischer, S., 1976, "Recent Developments in Monetary Theory," *Journal of Monetary Economics*, 2, 133-67.

Bartlett, M. S., 1935, "Some Aspects of the Time-Correlation Problem in Regard to Tests of Significance," *Journal of the Royal Statistical Society*, 98, 536-43.

Box, G. E. P., and Jenkins, G. M., 1970, *Time Series Analysis: Forecasting and Control* (Holden-Day, Inc., San Francisco).

Cagan, P., 1965, *Determinants and Effects of Changes in the Stock of Money, 1875-1960* (Columbia University Press for the National Bureau of Economic Research, New York).

Dwyer, G. P., Jr., 1976, *A Test of Fisher's Explanation of the Gibson Paradox for Pre-World War I Europe and the United States*, unpublished manuscript (University of Chicago and Federal Reserve Bank of Chicago).

Fama, E. G., 1975, "Short-Term Interest Rates as Predictors of Inflation," *The American Economic Review*, 65, 269-82.

Feige, E. L., and Pearce, D. K., 1976, "Economically Rational Expectations: Are Innovations in the Rate of Inflation Independent of Innovations in Measures of Monetary and Fiscal Policy?," *Journal of Political Economy*, 84, 499-522.

Feldman, S. J., 1974, "The Formation of Price Expectations and the Nominal Rate of Interest," Research Paper No. 7412 (Federal Reserve Bank of New York).

Fisher, I., 1896, *Appreciation and Interest* (The Macmillan Company for the American Economic Association, New York).

Fisher, I., 1930, *The Theory of Interest* (The Macmillan Company, New York).

Fishman, G. S., 1969, *Spectral Methods in Econometrics* (Harvard University Press, Cambridge).

Frenkel, J. A., 1977, "The Forward Exchange Rate, Expectations, and the Demand for Money: The German Hyperinflation," *The American Economic Review*, 67, 653-670.

Friedman, M., 1969, "Factors Affecting the Level of Interest Rates," in T. M. Havrilesky and J. T. Boorman, eds., *Current Issues in Monetary Theory and Policy* (AHM Publishing Corporation, Arlington Heights, Illinois) 362-78.

Friedman, M., and Schwartz, A. J., 1963, *A Monetary History of the United States, 1867-1960* (Princeton University Press for the National Bureau of Economic Research, Princeton).

Friedman, M., and Schwartz, A. J., 1970, *Monetary Statistics of the United States: Estimates, Sources, Methods* (Columbia University Press for the National Bureau of Economic Research).

Friedman, M., and Schwartz, A. J., 1976a, *Monetary Trends in the United States and the United Kingdom*, unpublished manuscript (National Bureau of Economic Research).

Friedman, M., and Schwartz, A. J., 1976b, "From Gibson to Fisher," *Explorations in Economic Research, Occasional Papers of the NBER*, 3, 288-91.

Frisch, R., and Waugh, F. V., 1933, "Partial Time Regressions as Compared with Individual Trends," *Econometrica*, 1, 387-401.

Gibson, W. E., 1973, "Interest Rates and Prices in the Long Run: A Comment," *Journal of Money, Credit and Banking*, 5, 450-53.

Gordon, R. J., 1973, "Interest Rates and Prices in the Long Run: A Comment," *Journal of Money, Credit and Banking*, 5, 460-63.

Gordon, R. J., 1976, "Recent Developments in the Theory of Inflation and Unemployment," *Journal of Monetary Economics*, 2, 185-219.

Granger, C. W. J., 1969, "Investigating Causal Relations by Econometric Models and Cross-Spectral Methods," *Econometrica*, 37, 424-38.

Granger, C. W. J., and Newbold, P., 1974, "Spurious Regressions in Econometrics," *Journal of Econometrics*, 2, 111-120.

Hall, R. E., 1975, "The Rigidity of Wages and the Persistence of Unemployment," *Brookings Papers on Economic Activity*, 6, 301-335.

Haugh, L. D., 1972, "The Identification of Time Series Interrelationships with Special Reference to Dynamic Regression Models," unpublished Ph.D. dissertation (University of Wisconsin, Madison).

Haugh, L. D., 1974, "Checking the Independence of Two Covariance-Stationary Normal Time Series," Technical Report No. 73 (Department of Statistics, University of Florida).

Haugh, L. D., and Box, G. E. P., 1974, "Identification of Dynamic Regression (Distributed Lag) Models Connecting Two Time Series," Technical Report No. 74 (Department of Statistics, University of Florida).

Hendershott, P. D., 1973, "Interest Rates and Prices in the Long Run: A Comment," *Journal of Money, Credit and Banking*, 5, 454-59.

Homer, S., 1963, *A History of Interest Rates* (Rutgers University Press, New Brunswick).

Jonung, L., 1975, *Money and Prices in Sweden 1732-1972*, unpublished manuscript (University of Lund, Sweden).

Kendrick, J. W., 1961, *Productivity Trends in the United States*, (Princeton University Press for the National Bureau of Economic Research, Princeton).

Keynes, J. M., 1930, *A Treatise on Money*, Vol. 2 (Harcourt, Brace and Company, New York).

Lucas, R. E., Jr., 1972, "Econometric Testing of the Natural Rate Hypothesis," in O. Eckstein, ed., *The Econometrics of Price Determination Conference* (Board of Governors of the Federal Reserve System and Social Science Research Council, Washington, D.C.) 50-59.

Lucas, R. E., Jr., 1973, "Some International Evidence on Output-Inflation Tradeoffs," *The American Economic Review*, 63, 326-34.

Lucas, R. E., Jr., 1977, "Understanding Business Cycles," in K. Brunner and A. Meltzer, eds., *Stabilization of the Domestic and International Economy* (Carnegie-Rochester Conference Series on Public Policy, 5, Amsterdam) 7-29.

Macaulay, F. R., 1938, *Some Theoretical Problems Suggested by the Movements of Interest Rates, Bond Yields and Stock Prices in the United States Since 1856* (National Bureau of Economic Research, New York).

McCallum, B. T., 1974a, "The Relative Impact of Monetary and Fiscal Policy Instruments: Some Structure-Based Estimates," *Journal of Econometrics*, 2, 283-99.

McCallum, B. T., 1974b, "A Small-Scale Neoclassical Macroeconometric Model: Estimates and Tests for Seven Countries," unpublished (University of Virginia, Charlottesville).

Meiselman, D., 1963, "Bond Yields and the Price Level: The Gibson Paradox Regained," in D. Carson, ed., *Banking and Monetary Studies* (Richard D. Irwin, Inc., Homewood, Illinois) 112-133.

Mitchell, B. R., 1962, *Abstract of British Historical Statistics* (Cambridge University Press, Cambridge).

Mitchell, B. R., 1975, *European Historical Statistics 1750-1970*, (The Macmillan Press LTD, London).

Mitchell, B. R., and Jones, H. G., 1971, Second Abstract of British Historical Statistics (Cambridge University Press, Cambridge).

Patinkin, D., 1968, "Wicksell's Cumulative Process in Theory and Practice," in D. Patinkin, Studies in Monetary Economics (Harper & Row, Publishers, Inc., New York).

Pesando, J. E., 1976, "Rational Expectations and Distributed Lag Expectations Proxies," Journal of the American Statistical Association, 71, 36-42.

Pierce, D. A., 1977, "Relationships--And the Lack Thereof--Between Economic Time Series, with Special Reference to Money, Reserves, and Interest Rates," Journal of the American Statistical Association, 72, 11-22.

Pierce, D. A., and Haugh, L. D., 1975, "The Assessment and Detection of Causality in Temporal Systems," unpublished (Federal Reserve Board and University of Florida).

Sargent, T. J., 1969, "Commodity Price Expectations and the Interest Rate," Quarterly Journal of Economics, 83, 127-140.

Sargent, T. J., 1973a, "Interest Rates and Prices in the Long Run: A Study of the Gibson Paradox," Journal of Money, Credit and Banking, 5, 385-449.

Sargent, T. J., 1973b, "Rational Expectations, the Real Rate of Interest, and the Natural Rate of Unemployment," Brookings Papers on Economic Activity, 4, No. 2, 429-472.

Schiller, R. J., and Siegel, J. J., 1977, "The Gibson Paradox and Historical Movements in Interest Rates," Journal of Political Economy, 85, 891-907.

Siegel, J. J., 1975, "The Correlation Between Interest and Prices: Explanations of the Gibson Paradox," unpublished (University of Chicago).

Sims, C. A., 1972, "Money, Income, and Causality," The American Economic Review, 52, 540-52.

Solow, R. M., 1957, "Technical Change and the Aggregate Production Function," The Review of Economics and Statistics, 39, 312-320.

Tobin, J., 1968, "Comment," Proceedings of a Symposium on Inflation: Its Causes, Consequences, and Control (Kazanjian Economics Foundation, Inc., Wilton, Conn.) 53-54.

Urquhart, M. C., and Buckley, K. A. H. (eds.), 1965, Historical Statistics of Canada (Cambridge University Press, Cambridge).

Wicksell, K., 1935, *Lectures on Political Economy*, Vol. 2 (George Routledge and Sons, LTD., London).

Yohe, W. P., and Karnosky, D. S., 1969, "Interest Rates and Price Level Changes, 1952-69," Federal Reserve Bank of St. Louis *Review*, 50, 18-38.

Zellner, A., 1975, "Time Series Analysis and Econometric Model Construction," in R. P. Gupta, ed., *Applied Statistics* (North Holland Publishing Company, Amsterdam) 373-398.

Zellner, A., and Palm, F., 1974, "Time Series Analysis and Simultaneous Equation Econometric Models," *Journal of Econometrics*, 2, 17-54.

Zellner, A., and Palm, F., 1975, "Time Series and Structural Analysis of Monetary Models of the U.S. Economy," *Sankhyā*, 37, 12-56.